OSPREY MILITARY CAMPAIGN SERIES: 44

PAVIA 1525

THE CLIMAX OF THE ITALIAN WARS

SERIES EDITOR: LEE JOHNSON

OSPREY MILITARY CAMPAIGN SERIES: 44

PAVIA 1525

THE CLIMAX OF THE ITALIAN WARS

ANGUS KONSTAM

First published in Great Britain in 1996 by Osprey Publishing,
Elms Court, Chapel Way, Botley, Oxford OX2 9LP,
United Kingdom.
Email: osprey@osprey-publishing.co.uk

ISBN 1 85532 504 7

Military Editor: Iain MacGregor
Design: Alison Myer

Colour bird's eye view illustrations by Peter Harper
Cartography by Micromap
Wargaming Pavia by Jim Webster

Filmset in Great Britain
Printed through World Print Ltd., Hong Kong

FOR A CATALOGUE OF ALL BOOKS PUBLISHED BY OSPREY MILITARY,
AUTOMOTIVE AND AVIATION PLEASE WRITE TO:

The Marketing Manager, Osprey Direct USA, PO Box 130,
Sterling Heights, MI 48311-0130, USA.
Email: info@OspreyDirectUSA.com

The Marketing Manager, Osprey Direct UK, PO Box 140,
Wellingborough, Northants, NN8 4ZA, United Kingdom.
Email: info@OspreyDirect.co.uk

VISIT OSPREY'S WEBSITE AT:

http://www.osprey-publishing.co.uk

KEY TO MILITARY SYMBOLS

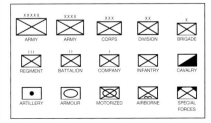

CONTENTS

THE FRENCH INVASION OF ITALY, 1524

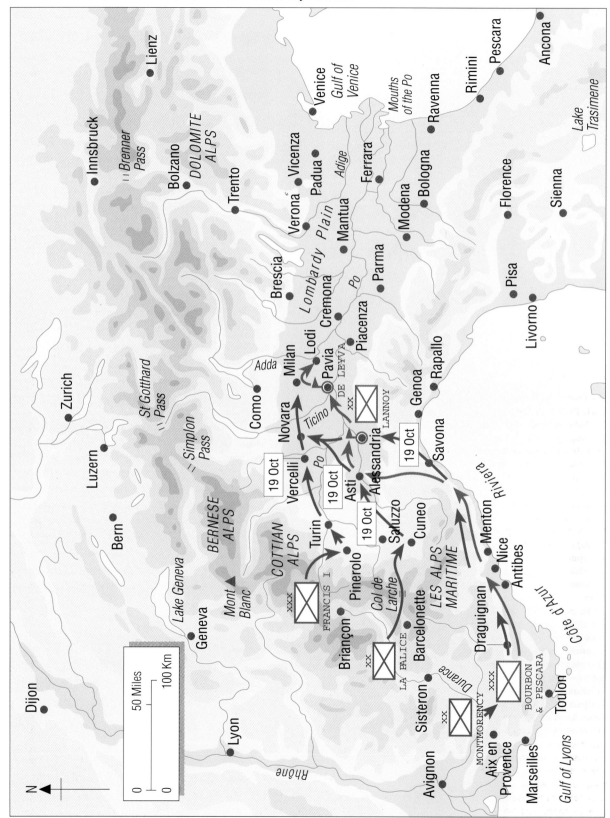

INTRODUCTION

Monsieur de la Palice est mort,
Mort devant Pavia,
Hélas! S'il n'était pas mort
Il ferait encore envie.

(16th-century soldier's song)

The French invasion of Italy, 1524. Following the failure of the Duke of Bourbon's Provence campaign and the arrival of the main French army at Marseilles, the Imperialists retreated back into Italy, closely pursued by the French. While the Imperialists retreated along the coast, Francis I and other French detachments crossed the Alps into Savoy, preventing any opportunity for the Imperialists to regroup and organise a defence west of Milan.

The positions of the three French bodies on 19 October 1524 are shown, when the Imperialist army were at Asti. This clearly shows the threat of encirclement facing the Imperialist army, forcing it to continue its retreat towards Milan. Lack of organised defences in the city and the threat of disease forced the Imperialist army to abandon the city to the French and to continue its retreat as far as Lodi. Imperialist garrisons remained at Alessandria and Pavia.

By 1525 France had been campaigning in Italy for over 30 years. Her original intention, in 1494, had been to enforce her claim to the Kingdom of Naples, but by the turn of the century her attention had focused on the more accessible and richer Duchy of Milan. The French armies were opposed or assisted at varying times by Italian states – either individual states or alliances, with both sides calling upon the support of Swiss, German and Italian mercenaries. In these campaigns France's toughest adversary was the Spanish army, and when the thrones of Spain and Austria were combined, in 1519, it altered the whole nature of the Italian Wars.

Between 1517 and 1519 the emperor Charles V inherited the ducal lands of Burgundy and the throne of the newly united kingdom of Spain. These were added to his traditional Hapsburg family lands in Austria and his loose control over the confederation of German states which came under the umbrella of the Holy Roman Empire. This created a cordon of potentially threatening Hapsburg lands which bordered France on three sides and meant that a French monarch would not just have to consider campaigning in Italy, but also expect attacks from Spain over the Pyrenees, from the Netherlands and from over the frontier with Germany. If these could be co-ordinated with an English invasion, France would be in an extremely dangerous position.

This was the situation facing the 20-year-old Francis I on his accession as king of France in 1514. During the following ten years France fought a number of campaigns in Italy as part of her greater struggle against the Hapsburg Empire of Charles V. The French were victorious at Marignano (1515) and met defeat at La Bicocca (1522), but by 1523 all France's previous successes in Italy had been undone, and Francesco Sforza, an Imperialist ally, held the Duchy of Milan. When Francis I gathered together his army for the forthcoming invasion of Italy, he knew that defeat would leave his country vulnerable to attack from Charles V and Henry VIII; victory would mean a reversal of fortune and the securing by France of Milan, the richest prize in Europe.

The Pavia campaign provides a fine example of the problems and decisions facing a Renaissance commander, and in the Battle of Pavia it provided the most decisive battle of the Italian Wars. Proclaimed as the first modern battle, Pavia saw the demise of the traditionally armed man-at-arms and the rise of the firearm as the arbiter of victory on the battlefield. The capture of the French king and the loss of the majority of his nobility marked the lowest ebb in France's fortunes since the Battle of Agincourt, over a century earlier. It also signified the end of the era of Swiss military supremacy and the establishment of the Spanish as the dominant military force in Europe, a position they would hold for almost a century.

Above all, the Battle of Pavia was the climax of the struggle between France and the Hapsburg Empire of Charles V, the superpowers of Renaissance Europe. It would ultimately swing the balance of power in Europe against France.

Albrecht Altdorfer, *"Baggage train and camp followers"*. Woodcut, c.1517. This clearly shows the impedimenta and baggage carried by an early 16th-century army. It was camp followers such as these who were attacked around the Castello Mirabello when it was seized by De Vasto's arqubusiers.

RIGHT **Guillaume Gouffier, Seigneur de Bonnivet, Admiral of France (1488-1525). A close friend of the king, whose advice the king favoured over that of his more experienced commanders. He was killed in the battle.**

ABOVE **Jean Clouet, Francis I, King of France (1494-1547), oil painting, c.1525. (Musée du Louvre, Paris) Regarded as the most powerful and chivalric prince in Europe, Francis conducted two campaigns in Italy: the first resulted in the French victory at Marignano (1515), the second ended in disaster at Pavia.**

THE FRENCH

Francis I, King of France (1494-1547), was crowned during the New Year of 1514/15, and within months began planning his first independent military campaign, which resulted in victory at Marignano in 1515. Throughout his reign he advocated an aggressive military policy, frequently attempting to break the perceived stranglehold imposed on his country by the territories of Charles V. In 1519 he was unsuccessful as a candidate for election as Holy Roman Emperor, but in 1520 he restored his prestige by staging the famous meeting with Henry VIII of England at the Field of the Cloth of Gold. Further setbacks, such as the defeat of a French army at La Bicocca in 1522 and the defection of Bourbon, only strengthened his desire to reclaim his title to the Duchy of Milan by force of arms, a policy which led directly to his defeat at Pavia.

Although criticised by modern historians for allowing court life and hunting to dominate much of his time, Francis I should be judged as a product of his time. In captivity following Pavia he wrote chivalric romantic poetry, reflecting an idealism that contrasted with the increasing professionalism of the Imperialist commanders.

A further major fault was his reliance for advice on his inner circle of contemporaries: he favoured men like Bonnivet and Montmorency over more experienced commanders. It appears that following the investment of Pavia he had no clear strategic plan, and blame for the poor disposition of his army around Pavia can only be laid at his feet; personal courage and knightly behaviour were insufficient virtues to ensure victory on the early 16th-century battlefield.

Guillaume Gouffier, Seigneur de Bonnivet, Admiral of France (1488-1525), was the king's closest friend. He had been brought up in court and had joined the household of Francis when the future king was 10 and he was 15. Both he and his elder brother, Artus, the grand master, had accompanied the king on the Marignano campaign (1515), where Bonnivet fought with skill and bravery. As with the king, war was not his only pursuit; he was described by Margaret of Angouléme (the king's sister) as being skilled in lovemaking (despite her veiled accusation of a failed rape attempt upon her by Bonnivet).

In 1518 Bonnivet led the embassy to England that resulted in the meeting between Francis and Henry VIII at the Field of the Cloth of Gold. He also took part in the canvassing for Francis' claim to the throne of the Holy Roman Empire.

During the Pavia campaign Francis continually sought the advice of Bonnivet rather than that of his more experienced commanders.

Robert de la Marck, Seigneur de la Flourance (1491-1537). A regular companion of the king and a trusted soldier, Flourance fought in several battles of the Italian Wars. At Pavia he fought with the Swiss, and was captured on the battlefield.

Bonnivet's courage on the battlefield was not matched by military knowledge, and his advice emphasised his impetuosity and chivalric idealism rather than the realities of the situation.

Robert de la Marck, Seigneur de Flourance (1491-1537), was another boyhood friend of Francis I. Born into an old Limousin family, Flourance had acquired extensive lands through marriage. Throughout his life he remained part of the inner circle of nobles surrounding both Louis XII and Francis I. He had participated in the battles of Ravenna (1512) and Novara (1513), and had been severely wounded in the latter. He had recovered in time to assist in the defence of Picardy against the English, and as a result had been given command of the French rearguard during the Marignano campaign (1515). As a reward for his valour he had been made Chevalier de la Main du Roi, and was regarded as one of the king's most loyal followers.

Flourance had been given the task of co-ordinating Francis I's unsuccessful bid to become Holy Roman Emperor, but had nevertheless been rewarded with the captaincy of the king's Swiss Guard. His close relationship with the king survived the defection of his father, the Lord of Sedan, to the Imperialist camp in 1518, and it was in his capacity of a commander of Swiss troops that Flourance took the field at Pavia. He was captured at the battle, and during his imprisonment in Flanders he wrote his *Memoires*. He was made a marishal of France on his release, and died following his successful defence of Peronne against the Imperialists.

Jacques de Chabannes, Seigneur de la Palice, Marishal of France (1468-1525), as one of the older group of officers in the French army, gave steady service despite being overridden in councils of war by the king's younger officers. He had fought in Louis XII's Genoese expedition of 1507 and had become governor of Milan in 1510. He had fought bravely at Ravenna (1512) in the cavalry vanguard, but on succeeding to the post of commander of the army had proved less skilful, and had been forced out of Italy. He had continued to campaign around Pamplona and Picardy, and took part in the abortive Battle of the Spurs (1513), again supervising the retreat of the French army. Despite this, he had been appointed a marishal of France in 1514 and had fought with Francis I at Marignano (1515). He had also taken part in the Battle of Bicocca (1522), where he had advised the French commander not to attack. As a brother-in-law of the king, Palice was considered trustworthy enough to crush any traces of the Bourbon rebellion, then to organise the defence of Provence in the face of the Imperialist invasion of 1524. During the Pavia campaign he held an independent command, although he fought with the king during the battle.

Jacques de Chabannes, Seigneur de la Palice, Marishal of France (1468-1525). An elderly and experienced commander by the time of the Pavia campaign, he was a great asset during the French invasion of Italy. He participated in the French cavalry charge at Pavia and died immediately after the battle.

Palice was noted for having a modern (non-chivalric) attitude to warfare, despite his age, and one wonders what the outcome of the campaign might have been if the king had taken his advice. He died shortly after the Battle of Pavia, and his death was recorded in a popular soldiers' song.

Anne, Duc de Montmorency, Marishal of France (1492-1567), was a favourite of the king, having been his boyhood companion. He had accompanied the king at the Battle of Marignano (1515), where he

Anne de Montmorency, Marishal of France (1492-1567). Another favourite of the king, Montmorency held the five abbeys with Swiss troops during the battle, but was unable to stop his men from routing. He was captured.

Louis de la Tremouille, Prince de Talmont, Marishal of France (1459-1525). He was the oldest and most experienced French commander at Pavia. A veteran of the Italian Wars, campaigns in Picardy, Burgundy and the Spanish border, his skills were widely respected by both sides. He was killed at Pavia.

had fought under Rene de Savoy, the king's illegitimate uncle. He had subsequently married Savoy's daughter, thereby strengthening his links with the king. Montmorency had been appointed first valet of the bedchamber in 1520, and following the Field of the Cloth of Gold that same year had led a diplomatic mission to England. On his return he had participated in the La Bicocca campaign of 1521/22, where his performance merited his appointment as a marishal of France in 1522.

At Pavia Montmorency commanded the five abbeys sector of the battlefield, where he was captured. Following his release he led the negotiations that resulted in the Treaty of Madrid, for which he was made grand master of the royal household. He became constable of France in 1538, but was banished from court three years later because of his support for a peace party. He was restored to court by Henry II and served in both social and military capacities during the early years of the French Wars of Religion. He died of his wounds following the Battle of St Denis, in 1567.

Louis de la Tremouille, Marishal of France (1459-1525), was the oldest and most experienced French senior commander at Pavia, though unfortunately his advice was rarely taken. La Tremouille was one of the richest noblemen in France, owning large estates grouped around his seat at Thouars. He was also the uncle of both Montmorency and Charles Bourbon. He had fought his first battle at St Aubin de Cormier (1488), and had subsequently served as a senior commander for three French monarchs. He had commanded part of Charles VIII's army which first invaded France in 1494, and fought at both Fornovo (1495) and the Garigliano (1503). Later he had commanded the French army during Louis XII's invasion of 1507, and also during the Novara campaign (1513), where his troops were defeated by the Swiss. He had been restored to favour following the accession of Francis I, and commanded part of the army at Marignano (1515). Following subsequent campaigning in Burgundy and Picardy he took part in the Pavia campaign, where he died in battle. Never an outstanding commander, he was nevertheless widely respected by both friend and foe for his age and experience.

Charles de Valois, Duc d'Alençon (1489-1525) was part of a disgraced branch of the Valois house whose links to the house of Orleans had risen with the accession of Louis XII. By marrying Francis I's sister, Margaret of Angouléme, he had been assured power, being the senior prince of the blood and in the line of succession. His first military experience had been during the 1507 campaign against Genoa, and at Marignano (1515) he had commanded the French rearguard. Alençon's performance had been less than satisfactory: his troops had broken under pressure and his division had had to be saved by Charles, Duke of Bourbon. Following campaigns in Burgundy he had given command of the rearguard during the Pavia campaign. During the battle he failed to support the king, and led the retreat of his troops back to Milan. Where today he might be thanked for saving at least part of the army, by contemporary standards his actions were seen as unchivalric, and he was branded a coward by chroniclers of the time. He died of pneumonia at Lyons following his subsequent retreat from Milan.

THE IMPERIALISTS

Charles de Lannoy, Viceroy of Naples (1487-1527), had been given command of the Imperialist army in December 1523, following the death of Prospero Colonna. The appointment had been made by Charles V more in recognition of Lannoy's social standing than his military ability (much as Eisenhower was appointed as supreme allied commander in 1942): Lannoy had the political and social skills required to unite the ambitions of the Duke of Bourbon with the military and political needs of Charles V.

Of Spanish origin, he held the title of Lord of Sanzelles, and had acquired his Neapolitan title in 1522. He had managed to keep the army together following the reverses of 1524, and had brought it within striking range of Pavia. During the battle he took direct command of the Imperialist cavalry, and was on hand to rescue Francis I from the Imperialist troops that surrounded him. Lannoy escorted the king during his period of captivity in Italy and Spain and took a direct part in the negotiations for his release, which resulted in the Treaty of Madrid. He returned to Italy to take part in the campaign of 1526/27 and later died in Naples.

Fernando Francesco D'Avolos, Marquis of Pescara (1496-1525), had

Fernando Francesco D'Avolos, Marquis of Pescara (1496-1525). One of the most gifted of the Imperialist commanders, Pescara co-ordinated the Imperialist response to the French cavalry charge and turned the tide of the battle.

been born into a leading Neapolitan family that maintained strong links with their Spanish roots. At 16 he had fought with the Spanish cavalry at Ravenna (1512), where he had been wounded and captured. Reportedly he had occupied himself during his year in captivity by writing poetry dedicated to his wife. On his release he had rejoined the Spanish army and campaigned in both Italy and Spain. During the 1521/22 Italian campaign Pescara had acted as one of the leading Imperialist commanders, and his troops had captured (and pillaged) both Milan and Genoa. He had also fought with distinction at La Bicocca (1522). He had assisted the viceroy of Naples in the defence of Milan during Bonnivet's invasion of 1523, and had subsequently been given the joint command of the Imperialist invasion of Provence (1524).

During the Battle of Pavia Pescara co-ordinated the movements of the main army as it entered the park, and his part in defeating Francis I and his cavalry was noted by Charles V. Wounded in the battle, Pescara convalesced in Milan, where he was approached by Papal representatives urging him to support a pro-French alliance. Despite promises of extensive Neapolitan lands, Pescara reported the alliance to the emperor. He died of a duodenal ulcer at the end of that year.

Charles III, Duc du Bourbon (1490-1527), was head of the leading noble family in France, a prince of the royal blood and the most powerful man in the kingdom after the king, holding extensive lands in central France. As the constable of France, Bourbon was the principal military figure, and had played an important part in Francis I's victory at Marignano (1515). A lawsuit against him by the king's mother had threatened a substantial portion of his estates, and this, combined with disgruntlement at his treatment by Francis, had led him to consider a revolt, assisted by Charles V and Henry VIII. When this had been discovered he had been forced to flee France and join the Imperialist camp. He had subsequently been stripped of his titles and his estates, and therefore had a major vested interest in the defeat of Francis I. He had proved an able commander during the Imperialist invasion of Provence (1524) and the subsequent campaigns around Milan which culminated in the Battle of Pavia. Although he took a minor role in the actual battle, the raid which escalated into victory owed much to his planning. Following Pavia he was granted the Dukedom of Milan as compensation for his lost French lands. This placed him firmly in the Imperialist camp, and it was he who led the Imperialist army against the Papacy in 1527, where he earned the sobriquet of 'the man who sacked Rome'. He was killed during the assault on the city.

Don Antonio de Leyva, Duke of Terranova (1480-1536), was already an experienced Spanish commander in 1525, having participated in earlier campaigns in the Italian peninsula and at sea. He commanded the Pavia garrison with great skill, melting down church plate to pay his mercenaries. Following the death of Pescara, in December 1525, he held the joint command of

Charles, 3rd Duke of Bourbon, Constable of France (1490-1527). Following his revolt against Francis I, Bourbon was forced to flee France and serve the Imperialist cause. His skill as a field commander was put to good use by the Imperialist army at Pavia and in the subsequent campaigns leading up to the sack of Rome.

Don Antonio de Leyva, Duke of Terranova (1480-1536). An experienced Spanish general, De Leyva held Pavia during the siege, where he repulsed all French attempts to assault the town. The sortie of the troops under his command during the battle did much to ensure the final Imperialist victory.

the Imperialist army with the Marquis de Vasto. He performed well during the campaign of 1526/27 that culminated in the sack of Rome, and continued to command the Imperialist army in Italy until his death in Milan following an abortive invasion of Provence in 1535/36. Terranova was of slight build, and for much of his life (including during the Pavia campaign) was plagued by severe gout. By the time of his death he had acquired a string of titles, including Prince of Ascoli, Duke of Newfoundland and Marquis of the Antilles.

Georg von Frundsberg, Lord of Mindelheim (1473-1528), was widely regarded as one of the most experienced field commanders of his age. In 1499 he had commanded the Imperial contingent in the alliance

Georg von Frundsberg, Lord of Mindelheim (1473-1528). A veteran Landsknecht commander, he fought in a number of battles in the Italian Wars, most notably at La Bicocca (1522). During the Battle of Pavia his troops defeated in turn Swiss, French cavalry and rebel Landsknechts.

formed to support Ludovigo Sforza, Duke of Milan, in his war with the French. His handling of Landsknecht forces serving the emperor Maximilian in subsequent Italian campaigns had earned him the sobriquet 'father of the Landsknechts'. He had been influential in the Imperialist victory at La Bicocca (April 1522), where he had fought pike in hand alongside his troops. This action had demonstrated that German mercenaries were no longer to be considered inferior to the Swiss, and had done much to enhance the Landsknecht reputation. Although in poor health at Pavia, his tactical abilities in controlling his troops enabled the Imperialists to move men to where they were needed. He did participate in later campaigns in Italy, but ill health forced him to retire to his estates, where he died in August 1528.

Alfonso de Avolos d'Aquino, Marquis de Vasto (1492-1546), had begun his military career as an aide to his uncle, the Marquis of Pescara. He had performed well during the Bicocca campaign (1521/22) and had assisted Pescara in the invasion of Provence (1524). Following the retreat of the Imperialist army to its camp at Lodi, he was given the task of reorganising the Spanish infantry and of increasing the proportion of arquebusiers, tasks which he performed adequately. His command of the raiding party at Pavia was partly a reflection of the standing he had within the army, although his exploits were exaggerated by his uncle in his report to the emperor. Following the death of Pescara, he was given joint command of the Imperialist army in Italy.

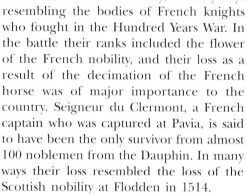

OPPOSING FORCES

FRENCH TROOPS

Cavalry

The French cavalry at Pavia was organised into lances, each comprising one gendarme, two mounted archers (in reality these were simply heavy cavalry; lighter versions of the gendarme), one coustillier (a lightly armed horseman), one valet and one page. The latter two were non-combatants.

The gendarmes were the aristocratic elite of the army, in many ways resembling the bodies of French knights who fought in the Hundred Years War. In the battle their ranks included the flower of the French nobility, and their loss as a result of the decimation of the French horse was of major importance to the country. Seigneur du Clermont, a French captain who was captured at Pavia, is said to have been the only survivor from almost 100 noblemen from the Dauphin. In many ways their loss resembled the loss of the Scottish nobility at Flodden in 1514.

The gendarmes were protected by good Italianate armour; the quality of the armour reflected the wealth and power of the wearer. Horses would also have been protected by barding, creating a heavily armoured combination of horse and rider.

While their principal weapon was a heavy lance, this would be quickly broken in battle and the gendarme would rely on a long sword, mace or war hammer for close-quarter combat. The half armour worn by the archers would be more of a munition quality, supplemented by mailed sleeves. His lance was also of lighter construction than that of the gendarme. Coustilliers, if treated as combatants were armed with a short spear, and operated as light cavalry and as general military dogs-bodies for their superiors. Their name reflects their lowly status and actual role: 'finishers off of the unhorsed'.

Anonymous. From the *Voyage de Genes* by Jean Marot, c.1510. French gendarmes with Swiss pikemen in the background attacking a Piedmontese frontier fortress in 1507. Note that the gendarmes are wearing their tunics over the top of their armour, with the exception of vambraces and gorgets.

ABOVE **Barnaert van Orley, The Pavia Tapestry (detail), c.1531. (Capodimonte, Naples) Charles, Duke of Bourbon, advancing, supported by Imperialist men-at-arms. His horse bard carries the barred Fleur de Lys, indicating his position as the senior French prince.**

OPPOSITE **School of Jorg Kolderer, Racks of Arquebuses in the Tyrol Armoury, watercolour, c.1507. An excellent depiction of the range of arquebuses in use during the Italian Wars. Some of those on the left are fitted with serpentines, the rest rely on the gun being touched off manually.**

Lances were grouped into tactical and administrative companies d'ordonnance of 100 lances. In action the French gendarmes would deploy en haie (in a single rank), with the archers and coustilliers (if used) forming subsequent ranks. The lances were the social and military elite of the army, and the strongest force in the French army.

Infantry

Unlike the cavalry, French infantry were considered inferior to those of other states. They were recruited into mercenary companies of around 200-400 men by professional mercenary captains holding a royal warrant. These adventuriers were largely untrained, and were drawn from the dregs of society. Pay was minimal, often merely sustenance, and the principal attraction appears to have been the opportunity of acquiring plunder. Of all the French infantry, those recruited in Gascony were considered to be of the best quality.

The infantry were armed for the most part with arquebuses, which were easy to operate and so required little training to use. The arquebus had replaced the crossbow as the principal French infantry weapon in the decade preceding Pavia.

Pikemen were also known in some mercenary companies. They were fielded as bodies of pikemen, often trained and led by Swiss mercenary captains. However, lack of success on the battlefield led to them being regarded as ineffectual.

The arquebusiers were formed into ranks of up to 12 deep, the pikemen in even deeper formations. At Pavia the only French infantry to take part was a group of Gascon companies who were stationed near the king. They proved unable to stop the Imperialist Landsknechts, who seemed to be able to scatter the French infantry with ease.

IMPERIALIST TROOPS

Imperialist Cavalry

Although at Pavia these may have included a number of German horsemen, the majority were 'Spanish', and as such could include troops from throughout the Spanish territories, including the kingdom of Naples and the bandes d'ordonance of Burgundy and the Low Countries. The cavalry were organised into lances, although these were smaller than those of the French: the Spanish version omitted the coustillier and one servant. With the exception of the Burgundian and Neapolitan lances, Spanish heavy cavalry were considerably lighter than their French counterparts, their horses were unarmoured, and their lance (lanza d'armas) was thinner and lighter than the French weapon. Traditionally, Spanish horseflesh was considered inferior to that of other countries, but by Pavia the army had been able to draw on supplies of good quality remounts from Italy and Germany, so this was no longer considered a problem.

German heavy cavalry was organised and equipped along similar lines, although from pictorial evidence they placed a greater emphasis on horse armour and carried a full lance (as did the Burgundian and French men-at-arms in Spanish service). All lances in the Imperialist army were organised into bandes d'ordonance (companies) of 100, although the pure Spanish companies appear to have been understrength. While the Spanish deployed en haie, German cavalry favoured a deeper wedge-shaped formation, a medieval concept adopted in the reforms of the emperor Maximilian.

The Imperialist army at Pavia contained a number of light cavalry, both Spanish ginetes and Italian mercenary stradiots. Both were armed with light spear and shield. The Italians also relied upon arquebuses, but the extent of their use dur-

ABOVE **Hans Schaufelein, Three Handgunners, woodcut, c.1513. Another depiction of Landsknechts to suit popular demand, this shows details of shot pouches and how arquebuses were shouldered. Note the figures are carrying slowmatch.**

Anonymous, The Battle of Fornovo, 1495, engraving (detail), c.1495.
A Swiss pike block at Marignano. The inability of the rear ranks to harm the enemy is clearly shown. Arquebusiers have deployed from the front of the unit to either side.

ing the campaign is unknown. By 1525 *ginetes* not only referred to pure Spanish light cavalry but also to those raised in the Kingdom of Naples for Spanish service. Although unable to stand up to heavy cavalry in battle (as was proved at Pavia), these troops made excellent skirmishers, raiders, scouts and general mounted workhorses for the army.

Spanish Infantry

Spanish infantry formed the most professional body of foot on the contemporary battlefield, being well trained, equipped and led. Those who participated at Pavia were to a large extent veterans, and according to

their commander during the battle (the Marquis of Pescara) they performed extremely well.

By 1525 these professional soldiers were organised in *colunelas* (columns), each of five *banderas* (companies). This gave a paper strength of around 1,500 men, commanded by a *coronel*. Four such units fought at Pavia, the troops recruited in Spain, Italy and the Low Countries. Each *colunela* was composed of pikemen, arquebusiers and sword and bucklermen (shield) roughly in the proportions of 2:2:1; the pikemen operated in a manner similar to the Swiss or Germans

and the arquebusiers formed into two bodies, each of 12 ranks deep. During the decade preceding Pavia the Spanish army had made a name for itself as the leading advocate of infantry firepower, and the proportion of arquebusiers to other troops was far greater than in Swiss or German units. This, combined with a Spanish superiority in field engineering, made them a superb defensive force. Sword and bucklermen, a particularly Spanish phenomenon, were trained to interpenetrate or work round the flanks of the pikemen when they had come to grips with the enemy, and to use their mobility to assist the pikemen in defeating the enemy.

Following Pavia, the Spanish infantry basked in a deserved glory, and for more than the next 100 years they were considered the finest troops in Europe.

MERCENARIES

The Swiss

The Swiss had built their military reputation on their defeat of Charles, Duke of Burgundy, in 1476. Essentially a pike-armed force, they had rapidly become known as the best mercenaries in Europe, and fought in the service of a number of states, including France, Spain, Milan and Venice. France in particular relied heavily on the Swiss to make up for French deficiencies in infantry. Their military reputation was based on skill and success, and they retained this reputation until 1522, relying on ferocity, training and professionalism to achieve the victory that their employer required. Following heavy losses at the Battle of Marignano (1515) and catastrophic casualties at La Bicocca (1522) their reputation became tarnished, and their place as the best infantry in

Melchior Feselen, *The Siege of Alesia*, oil painting (detail), 1533. (Alte Pinakothek, Munich) Imperialist men-at-arms en masse. These are formed in the deep wedge formation favoured by the Germans. They all wear Maximilian armour, more angular and fluted than the Italianate armour favoured by the French.

Europe was claimed first by the German Landsknechts and then, more convincingly, by the Spanish.

Although their principal weapon was the pike, anything up to a tenth of their number were arquebusiers, who formed a skirmishing line in front of the main body. At Pavia the Swiss mercenaries commanded by Flourance went into action without their supporting arquebusiers, a factor which may have played a part in their defeat.

The pikes formed into large bodies of up to 24 ranks deep. As with all pike formations at the time, only the front four or five rows could inflict any damage on the enemy; the remainder applied pressure, momentum and filled in any gaps. A small proportion of halberdiers were used to guard cantonal colours, or could be used to harass enemy troops in a similar manner to the Spanish sword and bucklermen described above.

The biggest problem with any mercenary force was that they demanded regular payment, not easy terms for contemporary commanders who had to rely upon intermittent supplies of money from

ABOVE **Barnaert van Orley, *The Pavia Tapestry* (detail), c.1531. (Capodimonte, Naples) Landsknecht arquebusiers in the foreground with a figure representing the Marquis de Pescara in the centre. Pescara is shown wearing Italian armour similar to that attributed to the Chevalier Bayard, now in the collection of the Royal Armouries, Leeds.**

RIGHT **The 22-year-old Francis I depicted at the Battle of Marignano (1516). He is wearing the up-to-date French armour, and clearly demonstrates the correct method of couching his lance. Although portrayed as bearded, the king remained clean-shaven until he was 25.**

their state coffers and poor administrative and logistical support. The phrase *'point d'argent, point de Suisse'* (no money, no Swiss) would have to have been constantly borne in mind .

At Pavia the Swiss mercenaries recruited by Francis I were not of the quality of those who were killed in such numbers at la Bicocca. Poor conditions, siege warfare and irregular payments did much to sap their morale, as was reflected by the abandonment of the army by a large body of Grison Swiss before the battle began. The Swiss at Pavia broke and ran from the field, something that had never happened with mercenaries who fought before 1522. Thus Pavia finally put paid to the notion of Swiss military supremacy.

Wolf Huber, Three Landsknechts, woodcut, c.1515. This excellent animated view is typical of a number of woodcuts by German artists featuring Landsknechts, a popular artistic subject in contemporary Germany. Note the soldier pulling up his stocking and the method of carrying pikes on the march.

OPPOSITE **Erhard Schoen, *The Siege of Munster*, woodcut (detail), c.1536. Demi-culverins of the early 16th century which clearly illustrate the style of contemporary gun carriages.**

The Landsknechts

Although employers might have regarded them as 'the poor man's Swiss' because of the superior Swiss reputation, these south German mercenaries were the most widely employed mercenary body in Europe. Established by the emperor Maximilian in 1486, they were initially created to form an infantry force within the Holy Roman Empire that was comparable to that of the Swiss. Units were raised by German military agents (often local rulers or landowners), and although they were required to swear an oath of allegiance to the emperor, when not required by the Empire these troops were hired out to other employers. Regiments of Landsknechts were organised into at least ten *Fahnlein* (companies), each of around 300-400 men. Although the principal weapon was the pike, a tenth or more of each regiment were armed with arquebuses, and acted as a protecting screen in a manner similar to the Swiss. Two-handed swordsmen and halberdiers performed the same function as their Swiss counterparts. From 1519 it was deemed an offence for Landsknechts to serve in the armies of enemies of the Holy Roman Emperor (i.e. France). Despite this, the French army at Pavia contained a regiment of 4,000 Landsknechts known as 'The Black Band', led by Georg Langenmantel. In battle they proved to be the toughest infantry in French service, and their ardour was probably heightened through being viewed as traitors by the Imperialist Landsknechts. As was the case when fighting the Swiss, neither side would give any quarter.

As mercenaries, Landsknechts caused the same financial problems

as the Swiss; De Leyva had to melt down church plate in order to pay those in the Pavia garrison. Although in Imperial service the tendency to return home when the money stopped was not as pronounced with the Landsknechts as it was with the Swiss, the riots after the battle bear witness to the financial headaches contemporary commanders faced when using any kind of mercenary troops.

ITALIANS

Derived from the Condottieri companies which had served for pay in the Italian states during the preceding centuries, Italian troops fought almost exclusively on a mercenary basis during the Italian Wars, even when fighting for their own state. By 1525 they were nearly all armed

Barnaert van Orley, The Pavia Tapestry c.1531 (detail). Capodimonte, Naples. French gendarmes in Italianate armour charging, with Imperialist landsknechts in the background. The leading figure represents Francis I.

with the arquebus, whether fighting on foot or on horse; both branches favoured skirmishing tactics. Although the 3,000 Italians (Neapolitans) were formed as a regular unit fighting in Spanish service, they were on contract, giving them a semi-mercenary status. They were also trained to fight in the Spanish manner, and were officered by professional Spanish officers.

The French army contained what was considered as the elite Italian mercenary formation of the period: the *Bande Nere* (Black Band*) commanded by Giovanni de Medici, son of Giovanni di Pierfrancesco de Medici and Caterina Sfortza.

Before entering French service, the *Bande Nere* had served the Pope and the Imperialist commander Lannoy, viceroy of Naples. Their defection from Imperialist to French service as a result of a pay dispute two months before the Battle of Pavia underlines some of the problems with mercenaries which have been outlined above. The force consisted both of mounted arquebusiers and arquebus armed foot, and those that remained in French service following the wounding of Giovanni de Medici took no part in the actual battle, since they formed part of the Duc d'Alençon's rearguard.

ARTILLERY

The first truly mobile train of field artillery is regarded as that of Charles VIII of France, employed when he invaded Italy in 1494, and the Battle of Fornovo, fought in the following year, was probably the first at which artillery played a significant role. The use of field carriages, limbers and horse teams was a novel concept at that time, but these mobile artillery trains became increasingly widely used during the Italian Wars (1494-1529), and at Pavia (1525) Galiot de Genouillac commanded a French artillery train of 53 guns of various sizes. The Imperialist army was accompanied by an artillery train of comparable size.

At Pavia the French employed their artillery to besiege the city, establishing two large siege batteries. A further battery of lighter guns were considered fine for use on the battlefield but too light to participate in a siege, and they were kept in reserve. The dividing line was drawn just above 'sakers' – guns firing a six-pound (2.7kg) ball, During the battle these light guns were stationed around the Torre de Gallo, but a siege battery which had been withdrawn to the area between Mirabello and the Porta Repentita contained larger pieces (demi-culverins and culverins). Both light batteries took an active part in the engagement.

Although during a siege where accurate gunlaying is important the rate of fire would be slow, on the battlefield a 'saker' could be reloaded in two or three minutes. At close range 'hailshot' (shards of flint or iron lumps held in a wooden frame resembling an hourglass) would be used to scythe through the ranks of oncoming troops.

---

* The name 'Black Band' was a common one used by mercenary groups, and should not be confused with the Landsknechts of the same name. In the case of the Landsknechts it is also said to have been adopted because of their blackended armour, and with the Italians it may be derived from a field sign of black mourning sashes worn following the death of Pope Leo X.

THE ORIGINS OF THE CAMPAIGN

F rancis I had intended to command the 1523 invasion of Imperialist-held Italy himself, but a major rebellion in France diverted his attention: Charles of Bourbon, the senior prince of the royal blood, had organised a revolt in his own feudal lands, and solicited the support of the emperor Charles V. The Imperialists had agreed to supply a German mercenary force to assist Bourbon's rebellion.

Bourbon's principal grievance against his monarch was that the king's mother, Louise of Savoy, Countess of Angouléme, had made an attempt to claim the greater part of the Bourbon heritage, which Bourbon had received through his wife (and cousin) Suzanne. The countess based her claim on being the next of kin to Suzanne, while Bourbon was only her second cousin. A lawsuit was fought through the courts, but the chancellor, Du Prat, was known to favour the king's mother.

Ludovico Corte, *The Principality of Pavia*, engraving, c.1654. This unusual map looks south and shows the park clearly. By this time the old and new parks were joined (the old wall where the breach was made having been demolished). San Angelo is shown in the bottom left corner.

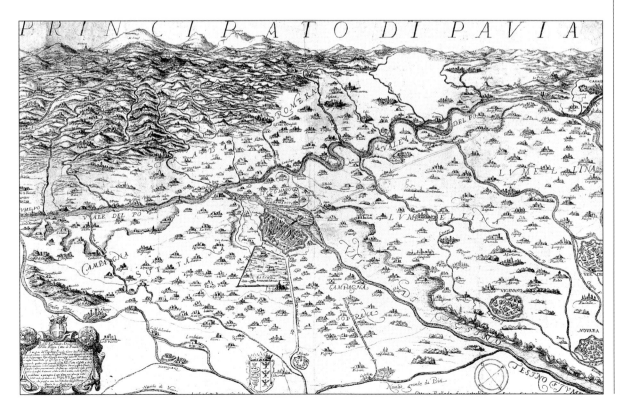

At the same time Francis I had refused Bourbon military commands which should have been his by virtue of his role as constable of France, and Bourbon decided to rebel rather than wait for the courts to strip him of most of his wealth and power.

Francis I's treatment of Bourbon may be explained by his certainty that he would in turn inherit the contested Bourbon estates, thereby improving his own personal financial position. The king was aware of Bourbon's discontent, but did not expect to drive him into open rebellion.

Bourbon's plans were discovered before they were completed, and he was forced to flee for his life into Italy, while the captains of his castles of Moulins, Chantelles and Carlat surrendered tamely at the first summons. Only some 80 gentlemen of his vassalage followed him across the frontier, so that he brought little practical aid to the emperor. His biggest assets were his position as a potential rival for the French throne and his extensive military experience. Both would prove useful to Charles V.

When the plot was uncovered, Francis I had no knowledge of how far the revolt might spread. He remained on hand to deal with possible uprisings and handed over the conduct of the invasion of Italy to his favourite, Guillaume de Bonnivet, admiral of France. While he was seeing to the security of his kingdom, Francis appointed his mother regent in his absence, and one of her first actions was to seize the Bourbon lands in the name of the king! Bourbon now bore a major grudge, and any chance of reconciliation had gone. Both Francis and his mother had made a dangerous enemy.

Ludovico Corte, Illustration of the City of Pavia (*Antiquissimae ac Celeberrimae / Regiaeq Civitatis Papiae Icon*), engraving, c.1599. This is one of the first examples of a prospective plan of the city, looking from the south. The abbeys of San Paolo, San Spirito and San Giacomo can be seen in the upper right-hand corner.

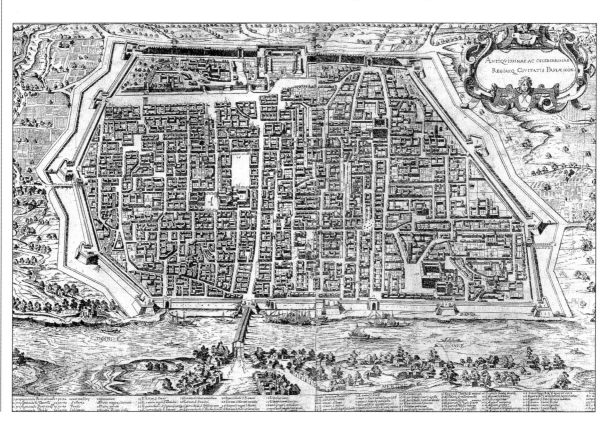

BONNIVET'S CAMPAIGN OF 1523/24

Admiral Bonnivet's campaign resulted from the Bourbon revolt, and although the main campaign narrative describes the events which followed it, a brief résumé is important. The campaign set the scene for Francis I's invasion of Italy in the following year. Although forming part of the French response to the concerted attacks from Spain and England, one of Bonnivet's primary objectives was to capture the constable of Bourbon.

Bonnivet entered Italy in October 1523 at the head of 18,000 French troops and with the finances to hire the same number again of Swiss mercenaries, who then joined him at Novara. His principal officers were the chevalier Bayard and Jean de Chabannes, Seigneur de la Palice.

Opposing him was the veteran Spanish commander Prospero Colonna with 9,000 men. As Bonnivet advanced towards Milan, Colonna fell back before him, but the French commander overestimated the strength of his opposition. He went into winter quarters between Milan and Pavia, allowing time for Colonna to send for 15,000 Landsknecht reinforcements. The latter was also joined by Bourbon with a further 6,000 Germans and money supplied by Charles V, and the Duke of Urbino also promised the Imperialists the support of 7,000 Venetians.

On 28 December Colonna died, and he was replaced by Lannoy, viceroy of Naples. While severe winter weather and disease killed off troops of both sides, Lannoy and Bourbon conducted raids against French outposts on the Ticino river and threatened the French supply lines. Faced with the prospect of being cut off from France, Bonnivet retreated towards Novara. Disagreements over pay led to 6,000 Swiss reinforcements refusing to join him, and when they

Jorg Breau, The Battle of Pavia, 1525, woodcut (detail), c.1526. Although crude, this gives a reasonable impression of the temporary defences erected around the Castello Visconti and the base of each tower in the city wall. Note the basic pillboxes used by besiegers and besieged.

Erhard Schoen, *The Siege of Munster*, woodcut (detail), c.1536. A closer detail of the type of circular earthworks depicted in a number of representations of the Battle of Pavia, including The Pavia Tapestry. Each has space for perhaps a dozen troops, and most appear to be pierced for arquebuses.

returned to Switzerland they took almost 13,000 Swiss troops from his army with them. The French were now heavily outnumbered and had no option but to conduct a fighting withdrawal towards the French border.

During an Imperialist probe led by Bourbon, Bonnivet was wounded, and Bayard and Saint-Pol assumed joint control of the army. Bayard commanded the rearguard during the withdrawal, and his death at the hands of a Spanish arquebusier has since been seen as symbolic of the decline of the medieval chivalric ideal and the establishment of gunpowder as the dominant force on the battlefield.

Saint-Pol and La Palice continued the retreat, reaching the French border at Briancon in April 1524. The Imperialist army occupied the Piedmont, with Lannoy establishing his headquarters at Alessandria. Imperialist control of Italy had been maintained, and Bourbon was still at large to prosecute his private war with Francis I.

THE PROVENCE CAMPAIGN OF 1524

Bourbon managed to convince Charles V that the Imperialist army was ready and able to carry the war into France, so a new campaign was ordered, supported by 300,000 crowns from the Imperial coffers. A force of 10,000 Spaniards, 800 Landsknechts and 26 guns was detached from the Imperialist army in Italy for the French invasion. This force, under the joint leadership of Bourbon and Pescara, skirted the coast, supported by the Spanish fleet. Crossing the border at Menton (near Monte Carlo), the month of July was spent sweeping through Provence, with city after city surrendering to the Imperialist army. On 9 August 1524 Bourbon entered the provincial capital of Aix-le-Provence and claimed the title of Compte de Provence. In this capacity he met the

Benardino Lanzani, View of Pavia, fresco (detail), c.1525. (San Teodoro Church, Pavia) One of two superb frescoes in the church, this detail is taken from the heavily damaged one which depicts the city during the battle. The Castello Visconti is shown in the centre, with a stylised representation of the park in the background. The park buildings have hesitantly been identified as the Toretta complex. The Porta Pescarina can be seen in the distance.

Melchior Feselen, The Siege of Alesia, oil painting (detail), c.1533. (Alte Pinakothek, Munich) This superb detail of 16th-century siege lines shows mortars in action in the foreground, waiting infantry behind them and a camp scene in front of them, protected from the defenders by a wagon line. The main siege guns can be seen in the upper left of the picture.

English envoy of Henry VIII, and swore allegiance to the English monarch in return for England's support in his claim on the French throne. What had started as a muddled political revolt had now become a fully fledged rebellion, with the rival to the French throne supported by a foreign army on French soil.

The only loyal French stronghold left in Provence was the city of Marseilles, which was invested in mid-August. Marseilles was defended by 4,000 troops under Mirandel, supported by 5-6,000 city militia. On 23 August a breach was made in the city walls, but the Imperialist assault was beaten back. It became clear to the defenders that it would only be a matter of time before the city fell, and while the Imperialists were calling up more guns and powder from their army in Italy, the defenders sent messengers to Francis I begging for help.

Meanwhile Francis had joined forces with Admiral Bonnivet and the remains of his army at Lyons. The French king knew the value of Marseilles: as an Imperialist base it allowed the enemy a foothold in France which could be supplied by sea. He called for more troops and marched south. By the end of August he had reached Avignon, where he waited for reinforcements.

By mid-September the Imperialists were ready to launch another assault on the city, but this too was repulsed with heavy losses on 21 September.

The Imperialists had now run out of options. Unable to take the city without incurring further losses and faced with a superior French army which was now advancing from Avignon, Bourbon and Pescara decided to retreat to Italy. Abandoning the siege and much of their artillery train, they fell back along the coast; the rearguard commanded by Pescara was harassed by the French advance guard led by Anne de Montmorency, constable of France. Francis entered Aix-le-Provence, hanged any collaborators and mopped up the province. By the end of

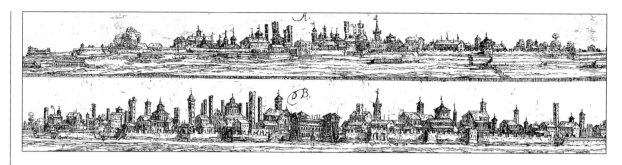

Ranutio Pratta, Siege of Pavia by the French, 1655, engraving, c.1656. The top view shows Pavia as it looked in 1655, looking south from the park. The lower view (B) is a representation of the same view as it would have looked in 1525, when the old medieval walls had still not been replaced by lines of ramparts and bastions.

Benardino Lanzani, View of Pavia, fresco (detail), c.1525. (San Teodoro Church, Pavia) The best-preserved fresco in the church, this detail is taken from a view of Pavia which is contemporary with the battle. The Castello Visconti is shown in the distance, while the foreground shows the medieval bridge over the Ticino river.

the month the Imperialists were back in Italy and the rebellion had been crushed.

FRANCIS INVADES ITALY

Francis now had the option of pressing his advantage and invading Italy or remaining in France (where his troops could influence the desultory campaigning by Lautrec around Bayonne). Influenced by Bonnivet he decided to follow the retreating Imperialists into Italy, where the prize of Milan appeared to be within his grasp. Financially, control of Milan would mean that the French could recoup their campaign costs.

Francis divided his army into several columns for the passage over the Alps. The advance guard, under Montmorency, was already pursuing the Imperialists along the coast towards Genoa; Michel-Antoine, the Marquis de Saluzzo, was at Briancon, gathering Italian mercenaries. The main body, led by the king, moved to join him, while a central column led by Marishal Jacques de Chabannes (La Palice) took the central route through the Col de Larche between Barcelonette and Cuneo. Part of the garrison of Marseilles followed Montmorency's advance in the fleet. The call also went out to the Swiss cantons for mercenaries to join the French army when it reached the Italian plains.

After a pause to go hunting around Sisteron, Francis reached Briancon on 14 October and linked up with the Saluzzo. October was not the ideal time to cross the Alps, but the main army struggled up and over the Col de Montgenevre, with the artillery train manhandled, winched and dragged along behind it.

By 17 October the main body had reached Pinerolo, 25 miles southwest of Turin, La Palice was at Cuneo and Montmorency had reached Savoy. The Alps had been crossed. The king continued on to Turin, where his uncle, Charles, Duke of Savoy, swore allegiance to his nephew. Francis halted only long enough to hunt and receive 14,000 Swiss mercenaries before pushing on towards Milan.

The military situation on 19 October was that Francis I with 24,000 Swiss, Italian and French troops was at Vercelli, half-way between Turin and Milan, while Bourbon and Pescara with 8,000 Spanish and 500 Landsknechts had retreated as far as Alba, 30 miles west of Alessandria, with La Palice's 7,000 French infantry and 2,000 men-at-arms hot on their heels. The Marishal de Montmorency, with a force of 5,000 mainly Italian light cavalry and Landsknecht mercenaries, was moving north from Savoy to cut off his retreat.

Papía

Mirabellū
garten
Thier

The Imperialists were in grave danger of being trapped between the three French columns. Fortunately for them, communication between the French columns was poor, and Francis I was unaware of the strategic situation. While the king crossed the Ticino river east of Novara, the Imperialists slipped out of the potential trap, Pescara force-marching with the Spanish to reach Pavia while Bourbon followed behind with the Landsknechts, who acted as a delaying force to hinder the Marishal de Montmorency. A garrison of 2,000 Spanish infantry was left to hold Alessandria.

The Imperialists now had garrisons at Alessandria and Pavia (which was held by De Leyva), and Pescara had established contact with the further small Imperialist garrison in Milan itself. Pavia was also the temporary headquarters of Charles of Lannoy, viceroy of Naples and Pescara's superior.

Francis encountered delays getting his whole army over the Ticino river, mainly because the medieval bridge at the crossing point collapsed under the weight of his artillery. Despite this, by 22 October his army was grouped around the small towns of Rosate and Abbiattegrasso, on the east bank of the river and only 15 miles from Milan. He had been joined by La Palice's column, who had managed to capture an Imperialist artillery train on the way while it was being moved from Novara to Milan via Mortara.

The French now faced two Imperialist forces: that of Lannoy and Pescara (now joined by Bourbon) at Pavia and the troops garrisoning Milan. The weather was atrocious, with heavy wind and rain, and while the main armies sheltered, both sides sent out reconnaissance columns to try to find out what the enemy was up to.

On 24 October one such column, comprising 5,000 Swiss mercenaries commanded by Jean d'Iespart (a French noble), ran into a force of 1,000 Spanish infantry billeted in the small town of Binasco, part of Lannoy's advance screen of troops. Although it was almost dusk, D'Iespart decided to attack the town, and fighting broke out as darkness fell. The fields around Binasco were broken up by irrigation ditches which hampered the Swiss, and the entrenched defenders proved difficult to dislodge. As Swiss casualties from Spanish arquebus fire mounted, the attack was called off. At this point the Marishal de Flourance arrived with reinforcements from La Palice's command, having marched at the sound of the guns. He surrounded the town as best he could in the darkness, and in turn called up La Palice, his superior, with his entire command. Francis saw the opportunity with which the skirmish presented him: with Binasco taken he could cut the line of communication between Lannoy and Milan, thereby creating the opportunity of storming the city with overwhelming numbers.

When morning came it was discovered that the Spanish had slipped away during the night. D'Iespart was sent after them, supported by Frederico de Bozzolo, an Italian mercenary commanding 600 light cavalry and 40 men-at-arms. They caught up with the Spanish near Scanasio, half-way to Milan, and in the ensuing skirmish the Spanish suffered heavy losses before Francis recalled the pursuers fearing that they in turn would be cut off by superior Imperialist forces.

Ludovico Corte, Pavia, engraving (detail), c.1617. The north-eastern corner of the city is shown here, and beyond the walls can be seen the abbeys of San Spirito and San Paolo, the Toretta and traces of the southern line of the park wall. The artillery bastions shown are all additions to the city defences erected after the battle.

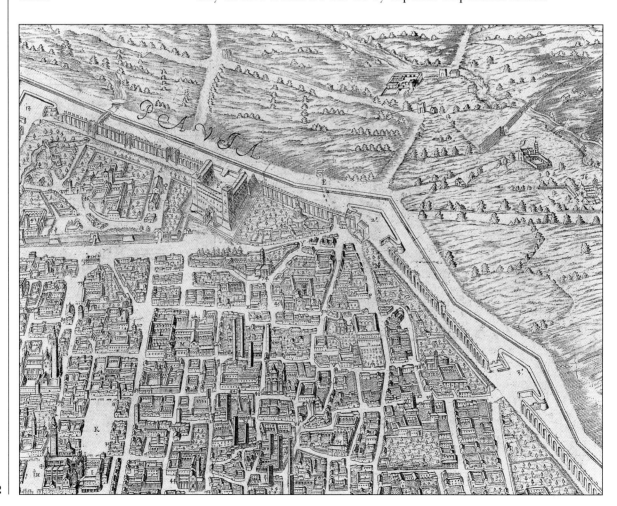

The bulk of the French army was now gathered around Binasco and Abbiategrasso, and while a third of the army held Binasco to prevent interference from Pescara, Francis advanced with the remainder towards Milan. French morale was raised on 25 October when the Milanese sent the keys of the city to the king.

Meanwhile the Imperialist army had managed to skirt around Binasco and entered the city on 26 October, joining forces with its garrison. Lannoy, in overall command of the Imperialist army, saw that the city was indefensible. Disease had decimated the city militia, the walls were in a poor state of repair and there was no stock of food in the city. Also, by now he was aware that he was heavily outnumbered by the French (approximately 16,000 Imperialists faced 33,000 French). The decision was made to abandon the city, and on 26 October the Imperialists began their retreat towards Lodi. Within hours French advance units led by the Marquis de Saluzzo and La Tremouille entered Milan and French cavalry then harried the Imperialist retreat as far as Marignano, where the pursuit was called off. Francis was now the ruler of Milan.

Modern military strategists might criticise the French monarch for not pursuing a retreating enemy with more vigour, but this was not a campaign fought on modern lines. He had achieved his objective of

Ludovico Corte, Pavia, engraving (detail), c.1617. This depicts the north-western corner of the city and the surrounding countryside, including the raised ground beyond the bend in the Naviglio stream, where some of the French artillery batteries were sited.

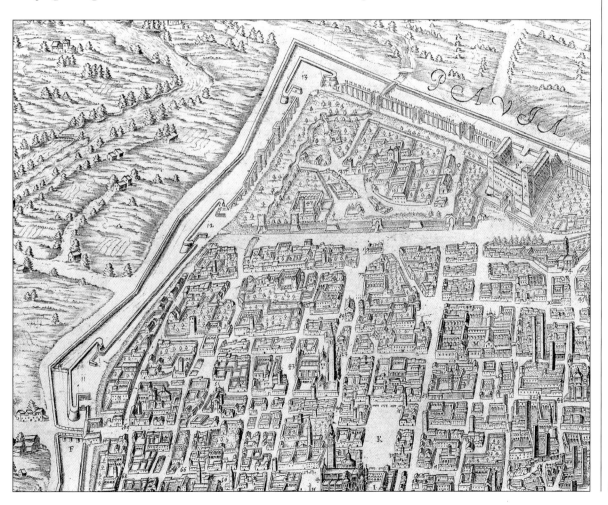

capturing Milan. His army had just conducted a successful winter invasion of northern Italy and was in need of a few days to recover. Francis was content that it did so outside the city, where a plague ravaging Milan would have a minimal effect on his men.

La Tremouille was installed as lieutenant governor of the city, where he was assisted by the Marishal de Foix and a garrison of 4,000 infantry and 600 men-at-arms. Within two days Francis was ready to resume the campaign and he called a council of war at Binasco. His older commanders, including La Tremouille and La Palice, favoured a direct attack on Pescara's army at Lodi, but Francis took the advice of the younger Bonnivet, who argued in favour of besieging Pavia, which was garrisoned by De Leyva. Bonnivet pointed out that a force there would be close enough to support Milan if the city was threatened. The order was therefore given to march south to Pavia.

THE SIEGE OF PAVIA

The French army was divided into a vanguard commanded by La Palice and Flourance, a rearguard under Charles, Duc d'Alençon, and the main body led by the king himself. Approaching the city from the north, through the Visconti park, La Palice stationed his Swiss mercenaries to the east of the city in the complex of abbeys, churches and monasteries and their handful of French infantry to the north, around the abbey of San Giuseppe and the Torre del Gallo. D'Alençon took up positions in and around the hamlet of San Lanfranco, to the west of Pavia, while the king, accompanied by his cavalry and the Landsknechts, moved into the centre and north of the park. The leading French units arrived on 28 October and the main investment took place during 30/31 October. The artillery train reached the city during the night of 31 October, and the heavy guns were divided into two batteries, one to the east and the larger to the west of the city. The lighter guns, which were of little use in a siege, were placed in an artillery park at the Torre del Gallo, with a further battery sited in the north of the park, where they could protect the king's encampment. Bombardment began on the following day.

While a pontoon bridge was being constructed over the Ticino river, to the east of the city, Montmorency was ferried over the river near San Lanfranco, with orders to invest Pavia from the south by occupying the area known as the Borgo Ticino. His force comprised 3,000 Landsknecht mercenaries, 2,000 Italian light cavalry, 1,000 Corsicans and 200 men-at-arms. At dawn on 2 November his advance guard of men-at-arms reached the bridge over the Gravellone stream, just south of the main city bridge over the Ticino. In the morning mist they stumbled across an artillery column accompanied by 500 Landsknechts under the command of the Count of Sorne. The 200 men-at-arms charged the column, capturing it and dispersing the infantry. The count and remnants of the Landsknechts managed to reach the Pavia bridge and so enter the city, but this last route into the city was effectively sealed off. Only an earthwork blockhouse remained in Imperialist hands on the south bank, and this was invested by Montmorency's troops. The only way Lannoy could relieve the city now was by defeating the French in battle.

Anonymous, Soldier with Jester's Cap, fresco, c.1530. (Turku Castle, Finland) The location of this representation rather than its content emphasises the degree to which the Landsknecht had become the universal mercenary soldier in Europe by the late 1520s.

During the first days of November a number of skirmishes took place as the two sides probed each other's defences. An attack was thrown against the small breach on the northern corner of the west wall, but this was easily repulsed; the French lost Claude, Duke of Longueville, in the process. A second attack at the same place was repulsed with substantial losses. A probe from the garrison by a unit of Landsknechts was in turn thwarted by Italian troops at the bridge over the Navaglio stream, where the road to San Lanfranco crossed the watercourse.

These skirmishes and bombardments were halted during 5-10 November, when heavy rain turned the area surrounding Pavia into a quagmire. The French took advantage of the weather to send to Milan and Ferrara for more powder (a commodity they were desperately short of) and both sides took stock of their situation.

De Leyva had a garrison of just over 9,000, the majority of whom were mercenaries. Only by seizing and melting down the church plate in Pavia could he guarantee that his troops would remain loyal. Food stocks were poor quality, but ample to allow the siege to continue for the foreseeable future. His real shortage was in financial reserves, and in the end this did more to bring about the battle than any other single factor!

On the French side the king realised that

Barnaert van Orley, *The Pavia Tapestry*, (detail), c.1531. (Capodimonte, Naples) The Castello Mirabello, the hunting lodge sited in the centre of the park, is shown here being stormed by De Vasto's arquebusiers. Note the bank and moat defences surrounding the castle.

OPPOSITE **Hans Suss von Kulmbach, Landsknechts, drawing, c.1508. (Albertina, Vienna) These depict early, unadorned military costumes. Despite the title, the figure on the right is probably a Swiss soldier. This is one of the best representations of a contemporary drum to be found.**

given the geography of the area, any co-ordination of attacks between the eastern and western entrenchment lines was well nigh impossible. The only area where both sides of the city could be observed at the same time was from the south bank of the Ticino river, the area occupied by Montmorency. The southern approach to the bridge was guarded by the small Spanish-held blockhouse, which was perfectly sited to act as a signalling station between the two French deployment areas.

When the rains were replaced by frost, on 10 November, the king decided to mount an operation to take the blockhouse and so allow co-ordination of his two siege batteries.

Montmorency's troops were reinforced by 1,500 French infantry and four culverins, personally supervised by Sissone, the French master of artillery.

The Spanish garrison of around 40 men was surrounded and bombarded with the culverins for most of the day before they surrendered. Montmorency ordered them to be hung, an action which produced strong protests from De Leyva and apologies from the king. The French now had complete control of the south bank and a vital communications post between their two encampments.

From this point on the bombardments intensified, and by mid-November a substantial breach had been made in the east and the west walls of Pavia. During this time De Leyva had not wasted his time, but had ordered that the citizens and militia throw up substantial earthwork barriers behind the city walls, fronted by a ditch, in effect forming an inner ring of defences with a killing ground between them swept by light artillery loaded with hailshot and arquebusiers. Unarmed militia stood by, ready to throw jagged chunks of marble down on the attackers.

ABOVE **Jorg Breu, *The Battle of Pavia*, 1525, woodcut (detail), c.1526. The foreground shows the northern wall of the park, with the Castello Mirabello on the far left and the western wall of the park in the distance. This print is perhaps the most geographically accurate of all representations of the battle.** ABOVE RIGHT **Hans Schaufelein, *The Battle of Pavia*, 1525, woodcut, c.1526. This bears little or no relationship to the battle, with stylistic representations of Landsknechts shown in rolling countryside. In reality the battlefield was completely flat.**

In addition De Leyva had constructed a string of small earthwork blockhouses around the city walls. Resembling modern pillboxes, these were designed to disrupt and unbalance any attack on the walls themselves.

Control of the blockhouse on the Borgo Ticino allowed the French to co-ordinate their assaults, and at dawn, probably on 21 November, two simultaneous attacks were made, one against each breach.

On the San Lanfranco side the king himself directed the attack, spearheaded by French bowmen and Italian mercenaries commanded by Marishal de Foix. Montmorency commanded an all-French second wave, which in turn was supported by Landsknechts led by the Duke of Suffolk and a count, Wolf. Three waves were sent forward in succession, and all ground to a halt in front of the inner earthwork. Co-ordination suffered when the king and his entourage joined the fight, and as the attacking force became pinned and disordered they were subjected to a devastating crossfire from the walls, entrenchments and blockhouses. Realising the situation was hopeless, the king called off the assault, leaving hundreds of dead and wounded in the killing ground, among which lay the standard of the king's Scottish Guard, which was captured by the garrison.

The assault from the western, five abbeys side was co-ordinated by Marishal de Flourance, assisted for the day by La Tremouille, who came from Milan for the occasion. Here the spearhead was commanded by Monsieur d'Aubigny and Bussy, and comprised volunteers and adventurers, including a large proportion of French noblemen. They were supported by further French troops under the Duke of Albany.

37

Flourance himself commanded the reserve, formed by the Swiss. D'Aubigny's troops were quickly repulsed, and their leader was wounded by a chunk of marble. As the first wave retreated they became enmeshed with the second wave, and both retreated in disorder. As Flourance moved the Swiss to the side to avoid them being disrupted, La Tremouille took charge of the retreating troops and called off the attack. Together the assaults cost the French over 800 killed and badly wounded. For the time being any further attack was ruled out.

With the assaults repulsed and the garrison busy repairing the breaches, the French commanders decamped to Binasco for a council of war. While his army licked its wounds, the king's military advisers recommended that he return to France, leaving one of them to continue the siege. This would keep his laurels untarnished and enable him to save face if further setbacks were encountered. Admiral Bonnivet argued that the king should remain and see the siege through to a successful conclusion. Flourance recorded that this was a 'double or nothing' gamble, because as the king's favoured commander, Bonnivet would 'be blamed and lose his credit'. He continued: 'The king places more trust in him than in the rest of the army.' Francis decided to continue to lay siege.

The French monarch now had to overcome a number of problems. First, ground conditions and the weather meant that the artillery bombardment of the city was less effective than it could have been. Flooded streams and meadowbanks prevented his artillery batteries from being placed near enough to the walls to do any real damage. One of the few exceptions was to the south of the city, where a small battery of guns on the Borgo Ticino managed to fire onto the city walls facing the Ticino river. These concentrated on the south-west corner of the city, where a tower and a section of city wall had been demolished. Secondly, his army was running out of gunpowder. Weather conditions meant that powder stocks were prone to water damage, and before the siege could be resumed with any vigour more powder would need to

ABOVE **Anonymous *"The Battle of Fornovo, 1495"* Engraving, c.1495 (detail)**
This detail shows the nature of field fortifications; in this case used by the Italians, but they resemble those which were constructed at Pavia by both the French and the Imperialist armies.

BELOW **Holbein the Younger, Infantry Battle, drawing, c.1530. (Kunstmuseum, Basle)**
Although this gives no indication of the national characteristics of the participants, it gives a very vivid impression of the nature of a struggle between pike blocks at close quarters.

be brought in. Messages were sent to the Duke of Ferrara, who had a virtual monopoly on black powder production in the Po valley.

Meanwhile, the siege continued. D'Alençon, commanding the rearguard of the army based around San Lanfranco, came up with the idea of diverting the Ticino river away from the walls of Pavia to allow an attack to be launched against the south-west corner of the city which was being pounded by the battery on the Borgo Ticino. This was to be achieved by damming the river opposite San Lanfranco and so diverting the water down the channel of the Gravellonne stream, which looped around the Borgo Ticino to join the Ticino river again just to the south of Pavia. Materials were gathered and boats impounded for several miles upstream from the city. The project involved mooring boats in a line across the river. Each boat was filled with stones, forming a series of deep-set pontoons. These were then joined with planks to form a semi-submerged bridge upon which the French labourers could work. Side skirts were fixed to the plank bridge, forming a tray, which was filled with more stones, so forcing the whole structure lower in the water. The surface of the tray was then planked over to complete a series of long boxes mounted on the boats which by now were completely submerged. The whole structure was then lined with heavily oiled sheepskins, nailed fleece inward, and anchored using cables and lead weights. The aim of the barrier was not to dam the stream completely (a feat considered impossible given the time, weather and available resources) but to cause the water level in front of the city to drop sufficiently for an attack to be launched along the riverbank. Despite being constantly breached and having to

be repaired, the barrier was initially successful in diverting some of the flow, but a week of torrential rain in early December swept the whole structure away and the project was abandoned.

It was probably this same torrential rain combined with the debris and extra flow caused by the collapse of the barrier that washed away the pontoon bridge which had so recently been constructed between the Borgo Ticino and the land to the east of the city. This catastrophe reportedly caused the deaths of numerous Swiss mercenaries and labourers who were struggling to save the bridge when it was swept away.

The siege was to continue throughout December and January, but lack of powder or poor weather often precluded the use of artillery, and the emphasis shifted from attempting to storm the city to trying to cause the defenders to run out of food and money. Desultory skirmishes and sorties continued, but increasingly the French looked elsewhere for a means of diversion

THE DUKE OF ALBANY'S EXPEDITION

On 5 December word reached the French command of a potentially dangerous development in Genoa, 60 miles to the south. Taking advantage of a split between pro-Hapsburg and pro-Vallois elements in Genoa, Don Hugo del Moncade, viceroy of Italy, had offered the pro-Hapsburg faction his support and troops. Any army landing near Genoa would change the whole strategic balance in northern Italy, so Francis had no option but to send a force to try to reach Genoa before the Spanish could land. He sent the Marquis of Saluzzo, who had local connections, supported by 6,000 men, including men-at-arms. Bad roads and poor weather delayed Saluzzo's march, and by the time he arrived at Voltri, near Genoa, he found that 3,000 men of a Spanish

Wolf Huber, *Battle before a Besieged Town*, drawing, c.1540. (Staatliche Kunsthalle, Karlsrue) This gives a good impression of the chaos involved during a sortie or assault.

force of 18,000 had already landed. While Saluzzo was approaching the landing beaches a powerful galley fleet commanded by the pro-Vallois Genoese naval commander Andrea Doria sortied from Genoa and drove off the Spanish transports. This left Moncade and 3,000 men stranded on the beach, and while they managed to hold off the French advance guard, the arrival of Saluzzo and his men-at-arms accompanied by friendly Genoese troops made their position untenable, and the Spaniards surrendered. The prisoners were marched into captivity in France, where they were paraded in front of the Queen Regent, and Saluzzo led his troops back to Pavia after ensuring the supremacy of the pro-French faction in Genoa. Francis could now concentrate his attention on the siege and the actions of the main Imperialist army.

Despite the Genoa operation, the campaign stagnated and reached a form of strategic stalemate. To break it Francis needed to woo the Italian states; any Imperialist reverse could lead to a number of states declaring for the king of France, and the Imperialist grip on Italy would be placed in jeopardy.

Principal targets were France's traditional allies, the Venetian republic and the Pope. In late November secret talks were opened with these and several other minor Italian states. Pope Clement VI intended to play both sides against the middle: while he was negotiating with Francis he sent 6,000 ducats to Lannoy in Lodi for the purchase of mercenaries for use by the Imperialist army.

On 12 December 1524 the Papal envoys signed a secret treaty with Francis, where they agreed not to aid the emperor Charles V or his forces, and to encourage other Italian states to do the same. In return they requested that France send a force to conquer Naples, then under Spanish control. Pope Clement's aim was not for Francis to accomplish this invasion but to use the threat of it to extract political concessions from the Neapolitans, and to strengthen the Papal State. In all probability the Pope didn't expect Francis to send any troops at all; rather the threat of an expedition would have been considered enough to help him

achieve his political ends. Against the advice of his senior commanders, Francis decided to send the Scottish Duke of Albany with 600 French foot, 4,000 Landsknechts, 300 light cavalry and 100 men-at-arms. Criticism that by acquiescing to the Pope's plea Francis was weakening the army was partly stemmed by the arrival of reinforcements. In the second week in December Giovanni de Medici (Giovanni of the 'Black Bands') arrived to offer his services to the French king. He was accompanied by a force of 500 light cavalry, 2,000 pikemen and 2,000 arquebusiers, all Italian mercenaries and considered to be the finest Italian troops available. He had just left Imperialist service due to lack of pay, so Francis I immediately paid and feted Medici's troops, and the troops swore loyalty to their new employer.

Lannoy in Lodi received word of the Duke of Albany's expedition, although he still did not know its purpose. Seizing the chance to raise the morale of his troops, he led a force comrising of 1,200 men-at-arms, 10,000 Spanish and Italian foot, 4,000 Landsknechts and 500 light cavalry to intercept him.

French scouts reported that the Imperialist army was marching south towards Piacenza, so a column comprised of Medici's 4,500 Italians and 4,000 Swiss

BREACH IN THE PARK WALL

The most suitable place to enter the park of Mirabello had already been determined by Imperialist scouts. Protected by the cover of darkness and later the early morning mist, the army reached its assembly areas in front of the park without being detected. Spanish engineers had already been sent to breach the wall, but by the time the army arrived the breach was still being made. Extra troops assisted them, but the extra noise produced alerted French sentries.

The scene depicts the main body of the army passing through the completed breach at around dawn. Imperialist officers supervised the passage and assembled their formations in battle order in the open woods beyond the wall. An advanced force of Imperialist arquebusiers had proceeded the main body, and it is surmised that another contingent secured and opened the gatehouse at the Porta Pescarina, increasing the speed of the passage into the park. While some accounts mention that the breach was large enough to allow cavalry and artillery access, others hint that the small Imperialist train of artillery entered the park through the Porta Pescarina itself.

Rupert Heller, *The Battle of Pavia, 1525*, oil painting, c.1529. (National Museum, Stockholm) One of the more accurate representations of the battle, the painting emphasises the fighting between Landsknechts on both sides. An interesting detail is the depiction of Imperialist troops in the foreground wearing their shirts over their armour.

commanded by Jean d'Iespart was despatched. The Frenchman commanded the column, with orders to force march until he linked up with Albany. Two days later, when the size of the Imperialist army was discovered, a third column was dispatched, led by Flourance, who was assisted by the Marishal de Foix. This force was made up of 8,000 Swiss mercenaries and 500 French archers.

The resultant weakness in the French siege lines was covered by the arrival of the 4,000 French archers who had been garrisoning Milan; these troops took the place of the Swiss in the five abbeys sector of the siege lines. This left only a handful of men-at-arms to hold Milan. It was felt that with suitable warning, reinforcements could be brought to them from Pavia, and given that Lannoy and the bulk of the Imperialist army was moving away from the city, the risk was considered acceptable. By this time La Tremouille, the lieutenant-general (governor) of Milan, was spending most of his time at Pavia rather than in Milan, as was his deputy, the Marishal de Foix.

As Lannoy crossed the Po river immediately to the west of Piacenza, D'Iespart caught up with the Duke of Albany at Fiorenzuola, half-way between Piacenza and Parma, where Albany was supervising the collection of powder and shot supplied by the Duke of Ferrara.

A fortified camp was constructed at Fiorenzuola, but when Flourance arrived with the third column, he found serious disagreements and bad feeling between the Swiss and French elements of the army. It took all Flourance's diplomatic skills and the special rapport he had established with the Swiss mercenaries to ease the situation. Resentment remained an undercurrent in the French army, and would continue when the troops returned to Pavia.

Lannoy was now moving south of Piacenza, with his army only 15 miles from that of Flourance. At this point he discovered that the Duke

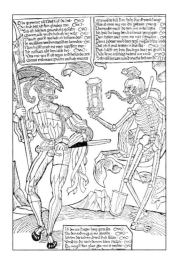

Anonymous, Death and the Halberdier, woodcut, c.1504. A crude popular verse sheet, emphasising the hardship of the soldier's life and the omnipresent threat of death.

Albrecht Durer, Siege of a Fortified Town, woodcut, c.1527. This extremely clinical impression of a siege is produced to emphasise the value of the modification of old medieval defences, in this case by the adoption of an artillery bastion. Even as early as Pavia, a Vauban-esque attitude to fortification was beginning to make itself felt.

of Albany's force had been reinforced and any chance of destroying a small element of the French army had been lost. In fact the French began an advance towards the Imperialists, and it became clear to Lannoy that he was outnumbered with his back to a river. He retreated to the Po river under constant harassment by the French, and sources are unclear if this was completely successful; it appears his army might well have been split, half reaching Codogno north of Piacenza while the rest retreated towards Cremona, north of the river but 17 miles further east. The retreat was conducted in fierce winter conditions and three feet of snow. The blizzards forced both armies to seek shelter temporarily, the Imperialists in Codogno and Cremona and Flourance's troops in the French camp at Fiorenzuola. The whole operation had cost the Imperialist army over 1,000 men killed, captured or wounded, and had done nothing to improve their morale. At Codogno Lannoy received the support of Bourbon, who had marched south with the Imperialist garrison from Lodi to cover the withdrawal.

When the storm abated the Imperialists regrouped at Lodi, and the Duke of Alba continued his march south to Florence; Flourance returned to Pavia, followed soon after by Medici's Italians, who were escorting a supply train containing powder and shot bought from the Duke of Ferrara. Christmas of 1524 found both armies back in their encampments.

The siege continued, and as the French thought that the city's capitulation was only a matter of time, the troops ordered from Milan refused to return north and miss their share of the booty. Their wishes were overruled, and the majority of the French archers returned to Milan disgruntled. Flourance retained perhaps just 1,000 of the most experienced, replacing in part the loss of a substantial detachment of Grison Swiss who had elected to return home to protect their canton from Imperialist plundering caused by the passage of Imperialist Landsknechts. The poor conditions endured during the siege and problems concerning leadership and pay were also strong contributory factors. Although the number of Swiss who returned home is unclear, some sources arguing that it could have been as many as 5,000, the effect on the army was evident; the attitude of the Grisons was symptomatic of the general demoralisation setting in, a situation made worse by the squabbling between the Swiss and French at Fiorenzuola. The

THE IMPERIALIST ADVANCE ON PAVIA, JANUARY 1525

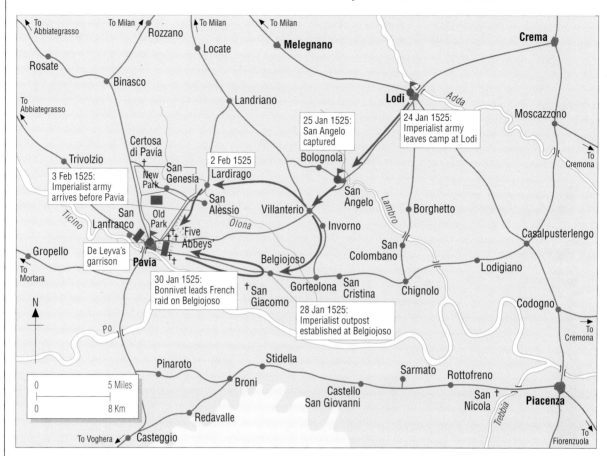

Following the arrival of Landsknecht reinforcements and money, Pescara felt strong enough to attempt to relieve the siege of Pavia. He quickly captured the French outpost at San Angelo which safeguarded French lines of communication between Milan and Pavia. An Imperialist detachment sent to Belgiojoso was attacked by a French raiding column, but the French returned to Pavia after the engagement, negating any advantage gained. The Imperialists continued their advance on Pavia via the town of Lardirago, arriving before Pavia on 3 February 1525. Prevented from reaching the city by the fortified French position around the 'five abbeys' (east of the cities), they entrenched in front of the French positions while its commanders decided what to do next.

effectiveness of the French army as a fighting force was slowly declining.

THE IMPERIALIST INITIATIVE

Back in Lodi, Lannoy was able to take stock of the situation. Any defeat such as that he had faced near Piacenza would mean that the whole of the north of Italy would be lost to the Imperialist cause. The fragile neutrality of states such as Ferrara and the token support of Venice would be overturned, and the French would be allowed to consolidate their hold on the Duchy of Milan. His army was too weak – and probably too demoralised – to undertake any significant offensive operations, but fortunately funding had been made available by the emperor through Austrian bankers, and Bourbon was sent north immediately before Christmas to collect the German mercenaries who were being gathered in Austria in the name of the Holy Roman Emperor. At Innsbruck Bourbon recruited the veteran German commanders Georg von Frundsberg and Mark Sittlich von Ems along with the 15,000 Landsknechts they had raised. In addition Bourbon collected 500 Austrian men-at-arms commanded by Graf von Salm and nine culverins from the Imperial arsenal in Innsbruck, together with ample stocks of powder, shot, supplies and gold. These fresh troops reached the

Imperialist encampment at Lodi on 10 January 1525 after force marching through the Brenner Pass. The guns and supplies arrived ten days later. The reinforcements breathed a new life into the army, and Lannoy, Bourbon and Pescara felt confident enough to consider going over to the offensive.

Castello de San Angelo was situated 11 miles west of Lodi and 25 miles from Pavia. It acted as an advance French outpost which could monitor activity in the Imperialist camp and give early warning of any

Giono tapestry Barnaert van Orley, *The Pavia Tapestry* (detail), c.1531. (Capodimonte, Naples) Swiss infantry and French gendarmes shown retreating across the pontoon bridge over the Ticino river. The construction details also resemble the description of the dam which was attempted early in the siege.

Georg Lemberger, *The War in Picardy*, miniature (detail), c.1512. (Albertina, Vienna) BELOW RIGHT Although produced 13 years before Pavia, this work illustrates the ferocity of a clash between pikemen, with ranks of men-at-arms in the background, Germans on the left and French on the right. BELOW The storming of a castle by infantry and men-at-arms, in this case all German troops. Note the pike block in the foreground is portrayed trailing their pikes, the standard method of transporting the weapon when not in action.

Albrecht Altdorfer, *The Terrible Swiss War*, miniature (detail), c.1515. (Albertina, Vienna) Another near-contemporary representation of pikemen in action, in this case emphasising the use of arquebusiers operating on the flanks of their parent body.

move towards Pavia. As early as mid-November La Tremouille had suggested to the king that a similar fortification in Melignano be occupied to perform the same defensive function for Milan; the pair would then have formed an advance perimeter protecting both cities. This plan was rejected by the king.

San Angelo was garrisoned by 2,000 foot and 500 light cavalry, all Italian mercenaries, commanded by Pirio Locque. Following the arrival of Bourbon from Innsbruck, La Tremouille sent him 800 Swiss Grison foot and 200 men-at-arms as reinforcements from Milan.

On 24 January 1525 the entire Imperialist army of almost 40,000 men marched out from Lodi towards San Angelo. The ground was frozen, allowing the easy movement of troops, and the castello was surrounded the following day. After a brief bombardment it surrendered to Lannoy; the Italian mercenaries were sent home on parole, and Pirio Locque and the Frenchmen were sent into captivity. Flourance's Swiss troops in the five abbeys had lost their advanced protective outpost.

While the bulk of the Imperialist army remained for two days at Villanterio, three miles to the southwest of San Angelo, before cautiously adavancing northwest to Lardirago, a Landsknecht column was sent south to Belgiojoso,

Barnaert van Orley, *The Pavia Tapestry* (detail), c.1531. (Capodimonte, Naples) Routing French gendarmes and other cavalry pursued by Imperialist horsemen.

48

Anonymous, *The Battle of Pavia, 1525*, oil painting (detail), c.1525-30. (Royal Armouries, Leeds) Spanish and Italian infantry passing through the breach in the park wall. The flags represent (from left) Bourbon, Sforza, Duke of Milan, the Holy Roman Empire and Spain.

eight miles east of Pavia. Their objective was to fortify the town and give early warning of any French move to cut the Imperialist army off from their base at Lodi.

Unable to save San Angelo and aware of the demoralising effect this might have on the French army, Francis decided to launch a disruptive raid on the Landsknechts at Belgiojoso. As this was not a major attack the operation served no strategic purpose, and the king's decision was against the advice of Flourance, La Palice and La Tremouille. Bonnivet supported the operation and so was given command of the mounted spearhead, which consisted of 400 men-at-arms. He was to be followed by Medici's Italians, supported by a further body of cavalry and 3,000 Swiss under the control of Flourance. After a confused skirmish Bonnivet succeeded in capturing the town with the assistance of

Anonymous, *The Battle of Pavia, 1525*, oil painting, c.1525-30. (Ashmolean, Oxford) Initially seen as identical to the Royal Armouries painting, the same artist has altered the composition of this copy (or original). French text labels have replaced the Italian ones, and the depiction of Mirabello is now in tune with other contemporary depictions.

Medici, and the remaining Landsknechts retreated towards San Angelo. In the late afternoon Bonnivet decided that the raid had achieved its purpose and he returned to Pavia, meeting Flourance's troops on the way. The Landsknecht garrison reoccupied the town during the night.

Meanwhile Lannoy and the main Imperialist army marched to Lardirago, with Bourbon commanding the vanguard and Pescara the rearguard. They entered the town at dawn on 2 February and informed the Pavia garrison of their proximity by firing their artillery pieces. Lannoy was now only four-and-a-half miles from Pavia.

At this point the French dispositions around Pavia were as follows: Alencon with the rearguard was at San Lanfranco; Montmorency's blocking force was on the Borgo Ticino, Flourance with his Swiss vanguard was in the area of the five abbeys and the king occupied the Visconti park with the rest of the army, including the cavalry, most of the Landsknechts, Medici's Italians and some Swiss troops.

During the day the Imperialist army led by Bourbon's vanguard crossed the Olona watercourse and entered Sant Alessio, a mile from the north-east corner of the park. They continued in column down the road leading

ARTILLERY BATTERY IN ACTION

When Charles VIII invaded Italy in 1494, he did so accompanied by a mobile train of artillery on wheeled carriages, heralding a revolution in the employment of artillery on the battlefield. Although once deployed the pieces were largely immobile, their impact, if correctly placed could be devastating.

During the battle of Pavia the use of artillery was limited to a bombardment and counter-bombardment between the Imperialist camp and the French guns at the Torre de Gallo, plus the chance encounter between the remainder of the French artillery train and the Imperialist infantry. The majority of accounts indicate that the Imperialist pikemen were fired on into their flank by the battery, which caused substantial casualties. However, the effect of this flanking fire was quickly negated by the charge of Francis I and his gendarmes which masked the fire of the French guns.

from Sant Alessio to the five abbeys, skirting the eastern wall of the park. This provided an excellent opportunity for the French to hit the Imperialist vanguard in the flank, but no such co-ordinated attack was ordered. The lack of French response was probably due to the heavy morning mist which screened the full extent of the Imperialist advance. The local French commander in the park launched a hit-and-run raid through the Torre del Gallo park gate with the 50 men-at-arms at his disposal. His troops caught a Landsknecht column in the flank and caused significant casualties before they retired back into the park. During the morning the remains of the Imperialist army was brought up and by late afternoon the army was established around the Casa del Levrieri, with outposts stretching north to Sant Alessio and south-east to Belgiojosio. The only other incident that day came at dusk, when Medici's Italians were ordered to move into reserve from the southern region of the park to San Lanfranco. Their move coincided with an Imperialist attempt to slip 50 Italian light cavalry into Pavia with supplies and orders. The two Italian units became intermingled in the vicinity of the Toretta, and the Imperialists were taken to be part of Medici's command. In the confusion the Italian cavalry managed to slip into Pavia.

That evening both French and Imperialist commanders had a lot to consider.

THE BESIEGER BESIEGED

By dawn the next day the Imperialists had brought up their artillery to the Casa del Levrieri and the guns were emplaced, part facing the wall at the Torre del Gallo and the rest facing the Swiss in the five abbeys. In response the French fortified the Torre del Gallo position, emplacing light guns behind an earthwork that ringed the farm. On the park wall side a firing position was built where six artillery pieces were able to fire directly at the Imperialists in the Casa del Levrieri. This developed into a daily exchange of artillery fire, the senior officers of both armies coming along for part of the day to see the 'black art' in action. At one point, about a week into the bombardment, Francis was knocked down by the blast from a barrage which reportedly killed a file of Swiss mercenaries who were standing near him. At around the same time, during a night-time raid, Bourbon attacked the San Paolo fortified complex from the direction of the bridge over the Vernavola stream. This attack was repulsed, but a second raid two nights later was far more successful. His troops slipped through the park defences near the Toretta and re-emerged through the Torretta gate to attack the abbey complex and the siege battery immediately to the west of the complex. He temporarily captured both positions, killing and wounding almost 400 of the Swiss garrison before a counter-attack by Flourance from the remaining abbeys using further Swiss troops forced him to withdraw, abandoning the captured guns. The battery was pulled back to the safety of Mirabello within the next few days.

The Pavia garrison increased its sorties from the city, concentrating on the San Lanfranco sector in order to tie down French troops as far from the main Imperialist army as possible. At this time the sector was held by Medici's Italian troops and French infantry commanded by

D'Alençon. In one of these sorties Giovanni de Medici was wounded in the leg, and Pescara granted him a safe passage to return home to Piacenza to recover. At a time when Francis needed all his available troops, one of his most able commanders was removed from the army, and a large proportion of his Italian mercenaries left with him. To make up the numbers, Francis recalled La Tremouille, Saint-Pol and approximately 2,000 troops from the Milan garrison.

Although all beneficial to the Imperialists, these actions did little to help the course of the campaign. By the third week in February the Imperialist command was forced to consider its rather limited options. To remain inactive meant that the army would disperse through lack of money. Poor weather and the strain of spending three weeks in such close proximity to the French army was having a detrimental effect on his troops, and casualties were mounting with no chance in sight of raising the siege. Money was also a problem for De Leyva in Pavia, and word was sent by him to Lannoy stating that he would be able to pay his mercenaries for only another few days, meaning that the city would inevitably be forced to surrender.

On 21 February, at a council of war, Lannoy said: 'In three days, four at the most, we must make contact with the garrison inside the town, or all is lost.' The Imperialist commanders realised that to retreat with the French so close was to invite defeat, as they considered that the French army outnumbered their own when in reality, both armies had around 25,000 men at their disposal. The time had come for to take action of some kind. It was considered that a direct attack on the French positions was not only foolhardy but would invite disaster, but some form of relief attempt would at least save face and allow Lannoy to claim that the offensive from Lodi had achieved at least some degree of success. This had the added attraction that such a raid through the enemy lines would demoralise the French army enough for the Imperialists to withdraw safely. This was the logic behind the planning which resulted in the Battle of Pavia.

Barnaert van Orley, *The Pavia Tapestry* (detail), c.1531. (Capodimonte, Naples)
One of several panels, this depicts the rout of the Swiss troops in the French army. The geography is wrong: the troops are shown fleeing towards the river to the west of the city rather than the east.

THE IMPERIALIST APPROACH MARCH

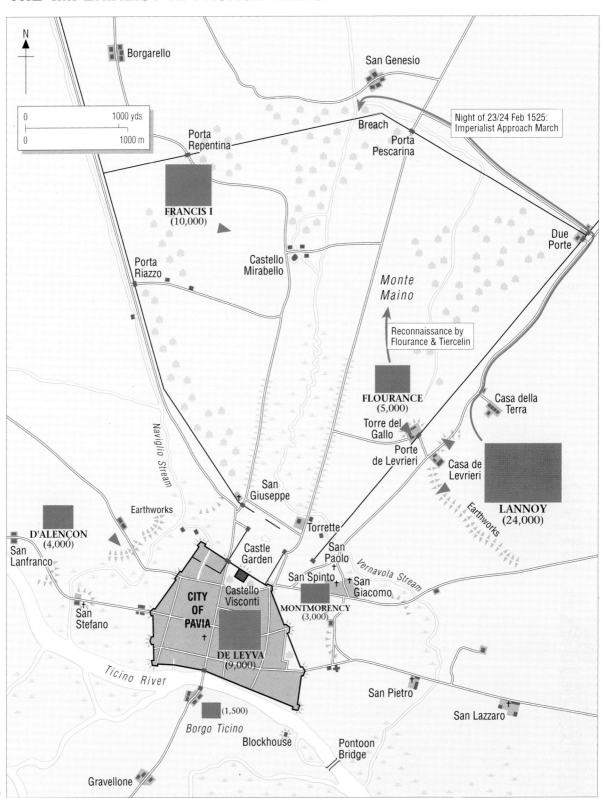

N

| 0 | 1000 yds |
| 0 | 1000 m |

Borgarello

San Genesio

Breach

Night of 23/24 Feb 1525:
Imperialist Approach March

Porta
Repentina

Porta
Pescarina

FRANCIS I
(10,000)

Due
Porte

Porta
Riazzo

Castello
Mirabello

*Monte
Maino*

Reconnaissance by
Flourance & Tiercelin

Naviglio Stream

FLOURANCE
(5,000)

Casa della
Terra

Torre del
Gallo

Porte
de Levrieri

Casa de
Levrieri

LANNOY
(24,000)

San
Giuseppe

Earthworks

Earthworks

D'ALENÇON
(4,000)

Torrette

San
Lanfranco

Castle
Garden

San
Paolo

Vernavola Stream

San Spinto

San
Giacomo

San
Stefano

CITY
OF
PAVIA

Castello
Visconti

MONTMORENCY
(3,000)

DE LEYVA
(9,000)

Ticino River

(1,500)

San Pietro

San Lazzaro

Borgo Ticino

Blockhouse

Pontoon
Bridge

Gravellone

THE BATTLE OF PAVIA
24 FEBRUARY 1525

THE PLAN

It was decided to conduct a raid into the park and seize Mirabello castle, thought to be the French king's headquarters. In fact Francis had moved his staff and court from Mirabello to the area around the Porta Repentita on 20 February, and the French artillery previously moved from the five abbey sector to Mirabello had also moved with him, forming a reserve artillery park of heavy guns half-way between the Porta Repentita and Mirabello. This area was also where the remaining Landsknechts in French service were stationed, near the mews reserved for the king's hunting birds, which had accompanied him on the campaign.

Once the Imperialist force had taken Mirabello (and, hopefully, captured the king), it would link up with a sortie northwards into the park by the Pavia garrison and so bring powder, food and whatever money could be spared back to Pavia. If they succeeded, they expected that the siege would have to be lifted.

As with the majority of such operations in the campaign, the raiding party would be supported by a second body, which would deploy in the park and pin any troops they encountered. The majority of the remainder of the army would provide a reserve, to be used in case the supporting troops got into difficulties, or to help extract the raiding force if the operation proved unsuccessful. A small force (perhaps 1,000) of Spanish infantry along with the remainder of the artillery held the original Imperialist positions around the Casa de Levrieri facing the five abbeys.

In order to allow any force into the park, a breach would have to be made, of a sufficient size large enough to allow formed bodies of troops to enter, including (if required) cavalry and artillery.

Over the previous few nights, starting on 19 February, Lannoy had sent patrols of Spanish engineers (guestadores) over the park wall to determine where a breach should be made and to try to find out something about French troop dispositions and the general lie of the land. These patrols all entered from the northern wall of the old park, and on 22 February a patrol reached the southern end of the wood facing Mirabello castle when it encountered a larger security patrol of Gascon infantry. Only three of the seven-man

Meemskerck, Francis I, King of France, at Pavia, engraving, late 16th century. An extremely unrealistic although widely reproduced version of the capture of the French king. The armour style is fictitious.

Hans Sebald Beham, *Baggage Train and Camp Followers*, woodcut, c.1530.
This train is depicted as being from Nuremberg, the wagon bearing the city crest. The Landsknecht costumes worn by the escort are similar to those worn by the Germans at Pavia.

School of Joachim Patinier, *The Battle of Pavia, 1525*, oil painting (detail), c.1527. (Kunsthistorisches Museum, Vienna) This detail provides a highly inaccurate and stylised impression of the capture of Francis I, with French gendarmes being forced off the battlefield by Imperialist cavalry.

Imperialist patrol escaped to report back, and further patrols were suspended for fear of causing alarm.

Following these operations the Spanish engineers reported that French security within the park was lax, and the area immediately west of the Porta Pescarina seemed to be the most suitable point to make the breach. In that section of the wall the engineers would be screened by a large wood, and once through, troops could move east along the wall and open up the Porta Pescarina to allow free movement of the supporting Imperialist troops. Reports vary as to the number of breaches in the wall – one, two or even three; in any event, they were made in close proximity to each other, and rapid passage of Imperialist guns into the park indicates that the gate was probably used.*

The plan was to breach the walls, send a force to Mirabello to link up with the Pavia garrison and protect these troops with a screening force comprising much of the rest of the army. The Imperialist commanders briefed their subordinates and preparations were made for the raid. On the night of 23 February all was ready. The following day, the feast of St Matthias the Apostle, was also the birthday of Charles V.

THE APPROACH MARCH

At around 10pm the Imperialists began their march north around the park wall, following the road to Lardirago. The troops were ordered to remain as silent as possible, and to identify friend from foe in the dark they were required to wear their shirts over their armour. If this was impossible, they were told to sew white squares onto their doublets. The only representation of the battle to depict this form of identification is the Battle of Pavia painting in the collection of the Livrustkammeren, Stockholm, where pikemen in the foreground are shown going into action wearing white shirts over their armour.

The force detailed to remain behind was ordered to engage the enemy at the Torre del Gallo and the five abbeys using arquebus and artillery fire, and to maintain camp fires to suggest that the bulk of the army had remained in the encampment. While this fire was to be maintained at intervals during the night, the guns were to cease their barrage before dawn. Then, their firing of three artillery pieces in succession

---

* Sources disagree on the location of the breach, and historians have suggested various locations: the most common are in the eastern park wall, south of the Duo porte (argued by Oman and Professor Casali), and the Pescarina area (supported by Thom and Giono). A detailed study of the battlefield combined with a close examination of the sources suggests that the latter is more likely this, combined with a military approach to any examination of the problems facing the imperialist attack came from the north of the park rather than the east.

as dawn broke was to signal De Leyva's garrison to sortie from the city in two directions; one small force would attempt to pin down the French on the San Lanfranco side of the city while the rest were to break into the park via the Toretta and link up with De Vasto's raiding party. The garrison were then to hold off any attacks from the area of the Torre del Gallo and the five abbeys while the raiders raced through their cordon and entered the city.

The bombardment began as soon as the main army marched away, and although its noise helped to obscure the sound of the move and the breaking down of the park wall, Lannoy had to send messengers back requesting that they fire with a little less zeal!

Charles Tiercelin, Lord of Roche du Maine, was in command of a French unit of light cavalry charged with the security of the park perimeter from the Torre del Gallo to the Porta Pescarina. He and his troops overheard the sounds made by the march north, and he sent French scouts over the wall to try to work out what was going on. Flourance, in his account, mentions that Tiercelin himself climbed the wall and saw the Imperialist army heading north, apparently trying to move as quietly as possible. Whether he concluded that they were withdrawing part of their force is unclear, but apart from alerting Flourance, who commanded the Swiss at the Torre del Gallo, Tiercelin took no further action.

While the Imperialist army was marching north up the Lardirago road, the Spanish engineers had begun their work on the breach. The location of the initial breach is unclear, but subsequent events indicate that the engineers were working to the west of the Porta Pescarina, in

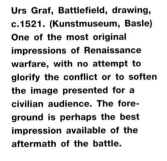

Urs Graf, Battlefield, drawing, c.1521. (Kunstmuseum, Basle) One of the most original impressions of Renaissance warfare, with no attempt to glorify the conflict or to soften the image presented for a civilian audience. The foreground is perhaps the best impression available of the aftermath of the battle.

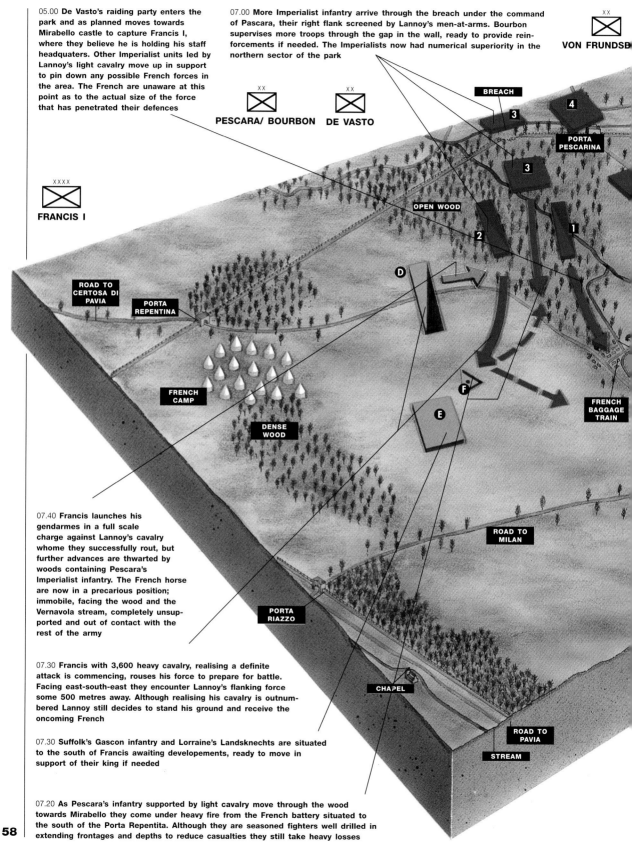

05.00 **De Vasto's raiding party enters the park and as planned moves towards Mirabello castle to capture Francis I, where they believe he is holding his staff headquaters. Other Imperialist units led by Lannoy's light cavalry move up in support to pin down any possible French forces in the area. The French are unaware at this point as to the actual size of the force that has penetrated their defences**

07.00 **More Imperialist infantry arrive through the breach under the command of Pascara, their right flank screened by Lannoy's men-at-arms. Bourbon supervises more troops through the gap in the wall, ready to provide reinforcements if needed. The Imperialists now had numerical superiority in the northern sector of the park**

VON FRUNDSB

BREACH

3

4

PORTA PESCARINA

3

PESCARA/ BOURBON

DE VASTO

OPEN WOOD

1

2

FRANCIS I

ROAD TO CERTOSA DI PAVIA

PORTA REPENTINA

D

FRENCH CAMP

DENSE WOOD

E

F

FRENCH BAGGAGE TRAIN

07.40 **Francis launches his gendarmes in a full scale charge against Lannoy's cavalry whome they successfully rout, but further advances are thwarted by woods containing Pescara's Imperialist infantry. The French horse are now in a precarious position; immobile, facing the wood and the Vernavola stream, completely unsupported and out of contact with the rest of the army**

ROAD TO MILAN

PORTA RIAZZO

07.30 **Francis with 3,600 heavy cavalry, realising a definite attack is commencing, rouses his force to prepare for battle. Facing east-south-east they encounter Lannoy's flanking force some 500 metres away. Although realising his cavalry is outnumbered Lannoy still decides to stand his ground and receive the oncoming French**

07.30 **Suffolk's Gascon infantry and Lorraine's Landsknechts are situated to the south of Francis awaiting developements, ready to move in support of their king if needed**

CHAPEL

ROAD TO PAVIA

STREAM

07.20 **As Pescara's infantry supported by light cavalry move through the wood towards Mirabello they come under heavy fire from the French battery situated to the south of the Porta Repentita. Although they are seasoned fighters well drilled in extending frontages and depths to reduce casualties they still take heavy losses**

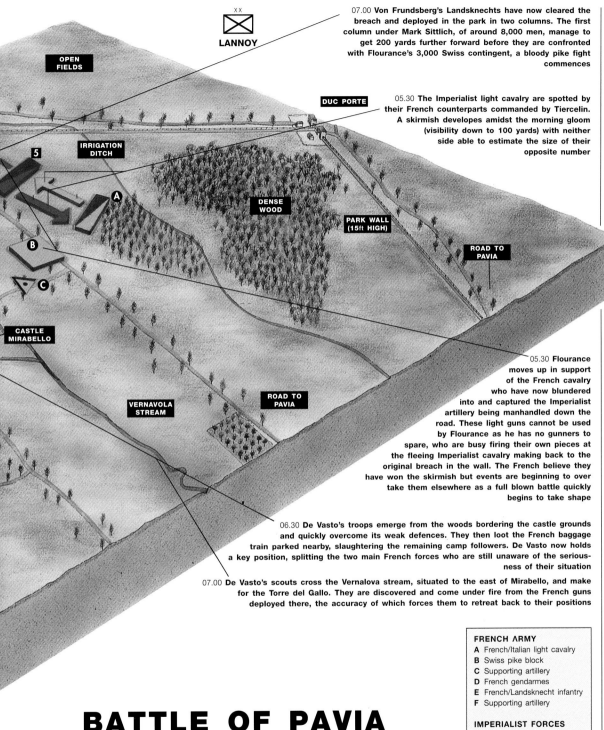

OPEN FIELDS

XX
LANNOY

07.00 Von Frundsberg's Landsknechts have now cleared the breach and deployed in the park in two columns. The first column under Mark Sittlich, of around 8,000 men, manage to get 200 yards further forward before they are confronted with Flourance's 3,000 Swiss contingent, a bloody pike fight commences

DUC PORTE

05.30 The Imperialist light cavalry are spotted by their French counterparts commanded by Tiercelin. A skirmish develops amidst the morning gloom (visibility down to 100 yards) with neither side able to estimate the size of their opposite number

IRRIGATION DITCH

5

A

DENSE WOOD

PARK WALL (15ft HIGH)

ROAD TO PAVIA

B

C

CASTLE MIRABELLO

VERNAVOLA STREAM

ROAD TO PAVIA

05.30 Flourance moves up in support of the French cavalry who have now blundered into and captured the Imperialist artillery being manhandled down the road. These light guns cannot be used by Flourance as he has no gunners to spare, who are busy firing their own pieces at the fleeing Imperialist cavalry making back to the original breach in the wall. The French believe they have won the skirmish but events are beginning to over take them elsewhere as a full blown battle quickly begins to take shape

06.30 De Vasto's troops emerge from the woods bordering the castle grounds and quickly overcome its weak defences. They then loot the French baggage train parked nearby, slaughtering the remaining camp followers. De Vasto now holds a key position, splitting the two main French forces who are still unaware of the seriousness of their situation

07.00 De Vasto's scouts cross the Vernalova stream, situated to the east of Mirabello, and make for the Torre del Gallo. They are discovered and come under fire from the French guns deployed there, the accuracy of which forces them to retreat back to their positions

FRENCH ARMY
A French/Italian light cavalry
B Swiss pike block
C Supporting artillery
D French gendarmes
E French/Landsknecht infantry
F Supporting artillery

IMPERIALIST FORCES
1 Imperialist advances guard (arquebusiers)
2 Imperialist cavalary (heavy & Light)
3 Spanish/Landsknecht infantry
4 Landsknechts with supporting artillery
5 Imperialist light cavalry

BATTLE OF PAVIA

24th February 1525 viewed from the south, showing the Imperialist entry into the northern portion of Mirabello Park, the initial French response, and the developing crisis as they are quickly split into three pockets of resistance each outnumbered by the Imperialists. (05.00 - 07.40)

N

the area screened by trees. They began work at 10pm, before the main army reached them, but by about midnight Lannoy arrived, having turned his army left into the new park just north of the Duo Porte. The new park wall posed no serious military obstacle, probably because the Imperialists had secured and opened the northern Duo Porte gate which led into the new park. From there a track followed the line of the wall towards San Giacomo and the Porta Pescarina.

Once at the breach, Lannoy discovered that his engineers were making little headway on the five-metre-high wall. The use of gunpowder was inadvisable because the noise of any explosion would wake the whole French camp, so Lannoy detailed off soldiers to assist the engineers and the work continued through the night.

By around 4am Tiercelin's scouts on patrol around the Porta Pescarina had reported strange noises, so he was aware that something was going on in the vicinity. He reported back to Flourance, who sounded the alarm and formed up a body of around 3,000 Swiss pikemen. While the remaining Swiss at the Torre del Gallo guarded the entrenchment complex there, Flourance ordered the majority of the lighter field guns at Torre del Gallo to deploy facing north, the direction from which the demolition noises were coming. He and his troops were still being confused by the artillery fire from the Casa del Levrieri, so any response was based on almost no information. In the end Flourance notified the king and led his 3,000 Swiss northwards towards the Porta Pescarina, accompanied by Tiercelin's light cavalry. By this time it was after 5am.

Not long before 5am the engineers working on the breach (or breaches) had lowered the wall sufficiently for the Marquis de Vasto and his arquebusier raiding force to enter the park. Keeping to the cover of the trees, they formed up and moved due south, towards the Castello di Mirabello. While various Imperialist sources record this force as being around 3,000 strong, with all arquebusiers carrying extra powder, shot, supplies and money, there is fundamental disagreement over the nationality of the troops. For apparently nationalist reasons sources argue whether the troops were Spanish, German or Neapolitan, but given the size of the Imperialist army and the proportion of arquebusiers recorded, it must have comprised around half of the entire Imperialist arquebusier force; whether they were detached from their parent units en bloc or detachments were provided from throughout the army is unclear. Operationally, it would make more sense if the unit had been formed exclusively from the unit of 3,000 Italian (Neapolitan) arquebusiers available to the Imperialist commanders, as was reported by Giacomo ad Capo.

While this was being done, engineers and small parties of troops moved along the wall and seized the other two gates, opening them to allow the rest of the supporting group to pass. Again sources are unclear about these actions: some suggest the gates were used; others that three breaches were made; and one states that the whole army traversed the one original breach. The latter action would have been impossible

Albrecht Dürer, *Siege of Hohenaspern*, drawing (detail), c.1519. An excellent contemporary representation of siege batteries, clearly illustrating the lack of standardisation inherent in artillery at this time. One of the pieces on the left is a bombard, a gun type that was considered obsolete by the early 16th century.

given the timing of subsequent events, and the three breach theory would also have delayed the army too long. The breach and gate solution appears to have been the most likely (and practical) course of action.

In any event, the first unit to enter the park was a battery of light field artillery; their orders were to provide support for the raiding party if they encountered problems storming Mirabello. They were followed by Italian and Spanish light cavalry, who deployed in the open ground to the south-east of the Porta Pescarina. (Another argument in favour of the gate theory is that for all three units to enter a breach, the wall would have to have been cleared to ground level, and the breach to have been at least three metres wide.) While the cavalry deployed in the open and began moving south, the artillery moved down the track that runs from the Porta Pescarina towards the point where it branches off to Mirabello.

As dawn was breaking and the darkness was being replaced by a thick mist, Flourance and Tiercelin were advancing northwards as De Vasto, the Spanish light cavalry and the artillery were moving south. The stage was set for a skirmish that would rapidly escalate into a full-blown battle.

THE SKIRMISH IN THE PARK

Tiercelin commanded approximately 1,000 French and Italian light cavalry, and around dawn he was leading them northwards from the Torre del Gallo towards the Porta Pescarina when he saw Spanish light cavalrymen through the gloom and rising morning mist. Visibility at

Anonymous, The Triumph of Maximilian I, miniature (detail), c.1519. (Albertina, Vienna) French prisoners in a variety of clothing are led into captivity by Landsknecht halberdiers. Note the astonishing variety of headgear, and the details of the Landsknecht costume.

THE IMPERIALIST ATTACK
(SITUATION AT 06.00)

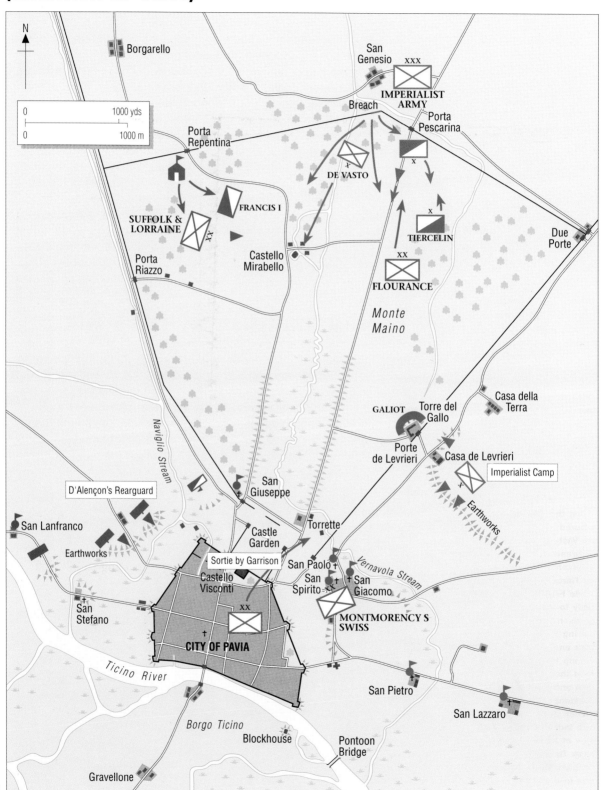

N

Borgarello

0   1000 yds
0   1000 m

San
Genesio   XXX
                           IMPERIALIST
Breach   ARMY
Porta   Porta
Repentina   Pescarina

DE VASTO
x   x

FRANCIS I

SUFFOLK &   XX
LORRAINE   TIERCELIN
                                          x
Porta   Castello
Riazzo   Mirabello   XX
                                     FLOURANCE

Monte
Maino

Naviglio Stream

GALIOT   Torre del   Casa della
          Gallo   Terra

          Porte   Casa de Levrieri
          de Levrieri
D'Alençon's Rearguard   Imperialist Camp
                                x
San   Earthworks
San Lanfranco   San
                       Giuseppe
Earthworks   Castle   Torrette
                  Garden
              Sortie by Garrison   Vernavola Stream
Castello   San Paolo †
Visconti   San   †   † San
               Spirito   Giacomo
San   XX   XX
Stefano   XX   MONTMORENCY S
         CITY OF PAVIA   SWISS

Ticino River

                         San Pietro
Borgo Ticino
         Blockhouse Pontoon   San Lazzaro
                     Bridge

Gravellone

62

this time (and indeed for most of the morning) was less than 100 yards. The two forces soon became embroiled in a series of mêlées, where neither side could really have been able to work out the size of the enemy. This clash would have taken place a few hundred yards south of the Porta Pescarina, between the track and the small irrigation cut which ran through that corner of the park.

At the same time, De Vasto's force was moving along the western edge of the woods leading to Mirabello, avoiding Flourance's Swiss, who must have passed within 100 yards of them as they moved up the road in support of Tiercelin's light cavalry. The Swiss had no idea what to expect up ahead, but were alerted to the presence of enemy troops by the sounds of the cavalry skirmish which was taking place ahead of them and to their right. As they moved forward they blundered onto the battery of Imperialist artillery being manhandled down the road. This column was quickly overrun: the Swiss captured between 12 and 16 light guns, and the Imperialist crews ran for cover in the woods and back towards the Porta Pescarina. Flourance's force was accompanied by a group of four light guns; these were now deployed and commenced firing into the mist, either towards the cavalry skirmish or directly towards the Porta Pescarina. It is supposed that these gunners were not sufficient in number to take advantage of the captured Imperialist pieces.

At this point Admiral Bonnivet appeared at the head of 50 men-at-arms, sent from the king with orders to find out what was going on. These cavalry and Flourance's Swiss now moved to their right, towards the sounds of the cavalry skirmish, and as they appeared through the mist the Imperialist cavalry broke, some routing east into the woods near the Duo Porte, the rest fleeing to their rear and the Porta Pescarina. Tiercelin regrouped his cavalry behind the small French gun battery and captured guns, while Flourance, fearful of being cut off by superior enemy troops, held his ground, facing north-west. Bonnivet returned to the king, reporting that an Imperialist incursion into the park had been repulsed. The time was now a little after 6am.

At around this time the guns at the Casa de Levrieri fired their three-shot signal to tell the garrison to begin their sortie. They then recommenced their bombardment of the Swiss positions around the five abbeys, firing blindly into the mist. This was enough for the local Swiss commander to put his troops on alert, expecting a dawn attack from the main Imperialist camp. When it came, the attack was launched from a completely different direction.

The garrison sortied from Pavia from the north-eastern city gate, heading for the gate into the park around the Toretta farm complex. The few French or Swiss troops on piquet duty there were quickly overwhelmed, and by the time the Swiss around San Paolo and San Spirito reacted, they found that the garrison was lodged in a secure defensive position which split the Swiss in the five abbeys from the rest of the army. While the Pavia garrison sent probes to the north to try to link up with De Vasto, the rest of the force harried the Swiss around the abbeys.

De Vasto and his arquebusiers were still some distance away. At around 6.30am they emerged from the woods just north of Mirabello and stormed the castle. Despite the noise of battle raging to the north-

When the main Imperialist army entered the park preceded by De Vasto's arquebusiers, Flourance led a body of Swiss pikemen to intercept, supported by Tiercelin's light cavalry. While Francis I called his main body to arms, the Imperialist garrison sortied from Pavia, seizing the southern end of the park and effectively cutting the French troops in the park off from their compatriots in the east and west of the city. By accident rather than design, the French army had been divided into four segments, each incapable of supporting any other body. By holding the central position, the Imperialist army was in a position to defeat each portion in detail.

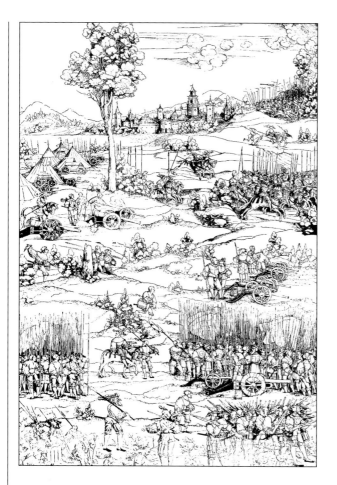

Hans Schaufelein, The Battle of Pavia, 1525, woodcut, c.1526. The second panel of Schaufelein's woodcut, this does at least include a representation of a pike block in action, with supporting arquebusiers in the wings. Clearly the clash between two blocks of Landsknechts caught the public imagination.

east, the handful of defenders must have been unprepared, as the castle was rapidly captured. Mirabello was also the park for the French baggage train and the attendant band of pedlars, artisans, prostitutes and camp followers. According to Flourance, those that were unable to flee were massacred by the Imperialists. The French army was now split in three: the Pavia garrison separated the Swiss in the five abbeys from the rest of the army and De Vasto's troops now occupied a position between Flourance and the king. Furthermore, nobody was really aware of where anyone else was; neither Lannoy nor Francis was aware of the true situation.

It was now 7am. De Vasto's scouts crossed the Vernavola stream, to the east of Mirabello, and moved down the track leading from the Porta Pescarina to the Toretta. As they drew level with the Torre del Gallo they came under fire from the French guns deployed there. The track there was built along a dyke which separated the ground around the Torre del Gallo from the boggy ground around the Vernavola stream. Unable to proceed under cover of the ditch because of the bog, and under fire from the French artillery, the patrols had no option but to turn back. At around the same time De Leyva's Pavia garrison was conducting a reconnaissance in force northwards between the Toretta and the Torre del Gallo. The Swiss defending the earthworks surrounding the Torre complex were on the alert, and soon another rather scrappy skirmish developed, this time somewhere to the south of the Torre del Gallo. It seems likely that some of the French artillery battery which had seen off De Vasto's probe would have turned their guns round and fired into the mist in the direction of the track leading to the Toretta.

While both De Vasto and De Leyva's troops were probing towards the Torre del Gallo, the Duke of Bourbon was busy supervising the movement of troops through the breach and the gates into the park. By 7am at the latest the Landsknechts commanded by Georg von Frundsberg and Mark Sittlich had entered the park in two columns. The first, of around 8,000 men (including approximately 1,000 arquebusiers), was led by Sittlich, and probably entered through the Porta Pescarina. It deployed to the open ground beyond the gate and after an advance of about 200 yards found itself up against Flourance's 3,000 Swiss pikemen. From contemporary accounts it seems likely that the Germans advanced in at least two large units or regiments, probably echeloned with their left flank block stepped slightly behind their companion block. Although the Swiss had a fearsome reputation as pikemen, many of their most experienced mercenaries had been killed at the Battle of Bicocca (1522), and Flourance's troops were not the veterans of earlier Italian campaigns. Both Germans and Swiss were demoralised due to lack of pay and the poor conditions of the previous few months, and both were led by commanders who, because of the mist, were not completely sure what was going on or what was required of them.

While this pike clash was going on to the south of the Porta Pescarina, a second infantry column entered the park through the breach. These troops were commanded by the Marquis of Pescara and numbered approximately 4,000 Spaniards and 4,000 German infantry. They were screened on their right flank by a cavalry force of approximately 400 Spanish lances of men-at-arms, with Lannoy himself at their head, supported by light cavalry. Ignoring non-combatants, this meant approximately 2,000 cavalry of various types. Bourbon remained in the vicinity of the breach, retaining command of the remaining Imperialist cavalry (probably Germans), rallying routers and stragglers and attempting to co-ordinate the various elements of the army.

The second column moved south towards Mirabello, ready to support either Sittlich's Landsknechts or De Vasto's Italian arquebusiers if the need arose. Both Francis and Lannoy imagined that they were still involved in a skirmish, and neither commander was fully aware of the tactical situation. In fact the Imperialists had not only split the French army into a number of small groups but had also achieved a numeric superiority over their enemies in the northern sector of the park by as much as three to one.

BATTLE COMMENCES

By about 7.30am the situation was as follows: Lannoy and Pescara, with around 8,000 and 2,000 cavalry respectively, were marching south from the park wall towards De Vasto, who held Mirabello with 3,000 arquebusiers. The remaining 8,000 Landsknechts were a few hundred yards to the east of them, on the far side of the central wood, and now facing Flourance, with 3,000 Swiss supported by Tiercelin's 1,000 French and Italian light cavalry.

To the west of Lannoy, at the Porta Pescarina, was Francis with around 900 lances of French gendarmes (3,600 combatant cavalry), 4,000 Landsknechts and 2,000 French (Gascon) infantry. An artillery battery was quartered to the south of his position. This meant that in this area the Imperialists enjoyed a three to two su-

School of Joachim Patinier, The Battle of Pavia, 1525, oil painting (detail), c.1527. (Kunsthistorisches museum, Vienna) A detail showing French earthworks thrown up in the five abbeys sector of their line, with a military camp behind them. The figures represent the rout of French troops from the battlefield.

THE STORMING OF MIRABELLO

The first Imperialist troops to enter the park were the force of Imperialist arquebusiers led by De Vasto. Their objective was to attack, seize and hold the main French encampment centred around the hunting lodge of Mirabello in the centre of the park. The lodge was built in the style of a small castle, surrounded by a moat fed by the waters of the Vernavola stream and protected by a drawbridge. The suprise achieved by De Vasto is indicated by the fact that the defenders were unable to raise the drawbridge over the moat before the Imperialist arquebusiers were upon them. The small garrison was quickly defeated, and fleeing survivors brought the news of the storming to the French king. The Imperialists had hoped to capture

Francis I in the raid, not being aware that he had moved his headquarters to the north-western corner of the park. The arquebusiers then looted the French baggage train which was assembled near the castle, and French chroniclers describe the massacre of camp followers (mainly prostitutes, traders and servants) which attended it. It is possible that this action was over-emphasised by the French as De Vasto was subsequently able to reorganise his men and join the battle with the French gendarmes when ordered by Pescara.

periority in numbers over the French, and the Imperialists held the central position.

In the south, French Master of Artillery Galliot commanded the 1,000 Swiss garrisoning the Torre de Gallo, supported by a substantial park of light artillery. A further 3,000 Swiss in the five abbeys sector were cut off from the Torre del Gallo by De Leyva's garrison, who sortied from Pavia with approximately 9,000 men. A further 1,000 Spaniards guarded the Imperialist artillery and encampment around the Casa del Levrieri. There were a further 5,500 French troops in no position to seriously influence the battle. These were the rearguard of 4,000 Italians and French around San Lanfranco and the 1,000 French infantry and 100 lances who held the Borgo Ticino. This rearguard was under the command of D'Alençon, who appears to have been on the Borgo Ticino when the battle began. The Imperialists therefore had a numerical superiority of more than two to one in the southern sector of the park and around the five abbeys.

As Pescara's troops moved south through the wood leading to Mirabello, they were screened on their right flank by the Spanish light cavalry and accompanying men-at-arms led by Civitas Sant' Angelo. As these two formations moved south, the gunners in the French battery to the south of the Porta Repentita caught glimpses of the Imperialists through the fog.

The number of guns in this battery has not been clearly recorded, but if we take it that the French had an artillery train of 53 guns, given the dispositions in other sectors of the battlefield, it must have been about 12 guns. The battery was deployed facing east, and although it couldn't move because of the surrounding sodden terrain, it was in a perfect enfilading position. At the same time, to the west, the small battery of four guns which had accompanied Flourance's Swiss column found the Imperialist foot in range to the north-west of their position. Both batteries opened fire. Once again sources are at odds when they describe the casualties inflicted by the French artillery: Pescara, who was on the spot, claimed that the artillery did little real damage, a version supported by Frundsberg, who was in the vicinity and fought on the same spot half an hour later; Moreau and Du Bellay both record that the guns performed carnage, and their accounts are accompanied by descriptions of arms and heads flying through the air. In reality, an early 16th-century battery firing at a range of approximately 400 metres against a force it could barely see and that was protected to some extent by trees would cause casualties, but not to the extent claimed by the French chroniclers. Both the Spanish and the Landsknecht troops in the Imperialist army were experienced, disciplined soldiers, and drills were in place for extending frontages and depths to reduce casualties from artillery fire. Thom (1908) estimates that casualties inflicted stood at about 600 men; this seems to be the highest possible figure.

The casualties caused by artillery fire would have been reduced by another factor: the nature of the clash between the French and the Imperialist cavalries. The French lances of gendarmes and supporting

Urs Graf, *Four Fifers*, drawing, c.1523. (Kunstmuseum, Basle) Swiss, French and German army musicians are shown here, emphasising the similarities of military costume encountered in the 1520s. If anything, the Frenchman is more ornately dressed than his Swiss or Landsknecht companions.

cavalry had prepared themselves and their mounts, and were ready to take part in the battle (authorities at the Royal Armouries of the Tower of London estimate that to be dressed in armour would take approximately 30 minutes). Swinging out of their encampment near the Porta Repentita, the entire force of around 900 lances deployed in line facing east-south-east. If we omit the non-combatants from the lance organisation, this gives a force of around 3,600 men, comprising gendarmes, archers (heavy cavalry) and coustilliers (light cavalry), deployed in four ranks, with the gendarmes in the front line. Although a tactical unit comprised 100 lances, at Pavia the entire force charged as one body, with no reserves or supporting infantry. In this respect the French cavalry resembled their ancestors at Crécy, Poitiers and Agincourt.

To their front were the flanking cavalry force of the Imperialist army, now riding south in column to the west of the wood, approximately 500 metres away. This was a mixed force of approximately 500 ginetes (Spanish light cavalry) led by Civitas Sant' Angelo and 400 lances of Spanish heavy cavalry (1,600 horsemen) commanded by Lannoy. Although they were heavily outnumbered and outclassed (Spanish men-at-arms were noted as being less well armoured than their French counterparts), Lannoy wheeled his horsemen into line facing the French threat. Reputedly, Lannoy faced this unequal struggle with the words: 'There is no hope left except in God.' Francis ordered his lances to advance, blocking the fire of his artillery, and his lances built up speed as they approached the enemy. Given that the Imperialist horse advanced in response, the charge took approximately three minutes, and the subsequent clash of horsemen about the same time again.

The Imperialist cavalry were quickly scattered, and Sant' Angelo was killed in the clash. They routed to the east or south-east, towards the cover of the wood and their supporting infantry. The French king and his lances pursued, reining in at the edge of the wood, approximately 600 yards from their starting positions. They had broken the Imperialist horse; the only troops in their vicinity were Imperialist infantry, who had run for the cover of the trees on their approach. At this point Francis is reputed to have turned to the Marishal de Foix and said: 'Monsieur de Lescun, now I really am the Duke of Milan.'

Francis believed he had won the battle. He had cleared the ground of Imperialists and penned them up in a wood. His latest report from the east came from Bonnivet, and indicated that Flourance was in charge of the situation. Although he had received no word from Montmorency and Alençon, Francis had no reason to think that the situation south of his position was precarious, and he remained unaware of the sortie of De Leyva's Pavia garrison. In fact his horsemen were now completely unsupported, facing a wood and the Vernavola stream, and out of contact with the rest of the army.

Although Lannoy had been carried off with the routing Imperialist horse, Pescara was on hand and took charge of the situation. If he could bring up sufficient infantry before the French cavalry had time to regroup and reorganise themselves, he felt he had a chance to defeat them in detail. He recalled De Vasto and his 3,000 arquebusiers, ordering them to fall on the French right flank, where they would be partly protected by the irrigation ditches around Mirabello. While he sent messengers to Bourbon and Frundsberg requesting support, he

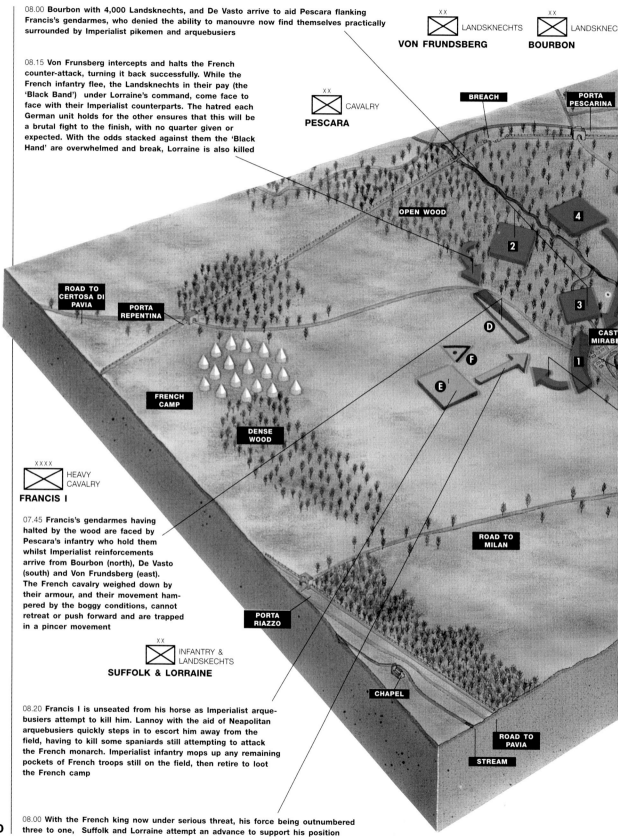

08.00 **Bourbon with 4,000 Landsknechts, and De Vasto arrive to aid Pescara flanking Francis's gendarmes, who denied the ability to manouvre now find themselves practically surrounded by Imperialist pikemen and arquebusiers**

08.15 **Von Frunsberg intercepts and halts the French counter-attack, turning it back successfully. While the French infantry flee, the Landsknechts in their pay (the 'Black Band') under Lorraine's command, come face to face with their Imperialist counterparts. The hatred each German unit holds for the other ensures that this will be a brutal fight to the finish, with no quarter given or expected. With the odds stacked against them the 'Black Hand' are overwhelmed and break, Lorraine is also killed**

x x
⊠ LANDSKNECHTS
VON FRUNDSBERG

x x
⊠ LANDSKNEC
BOURBON

x x
⊠ CAVALRY
PESCARA

BREACH

PORTA PESCARINA

OPEN WOOD

4

2

ROAD TO CERTOSA DI PAVIA

PORTA REPENTINA

3

D

CAST MIRAB

F

1

E

FRENCH CAMP

x x x x
⊠ HEAVY CAVALRY
FRANCIS I

DENSE WOOD

07.45 **Francis's gendarmes having halted by the wood are faced by Pescara's infantry who hold them whilst Imperialist reinforcements arrive from Bourbon (north), De Vasto (south) and Von Frundsberg (east). The French cavalry weighed down by their armour, and their movement hampered by the boggy conditions, cannot retreat or push forward and are trapped in a pincer movement**

ROAD TO MILAN

x x
⊠ INFANTRY & LANDSKECHTS
SUFFOLK & LORRAINE

PORTA RIAZZO

CHAPEL

08.20 **Francis I is unseated from his horse as Imperialist arquebusiers attempt to kill him. Lannoy with the aid of Neapolitan arquebusiers quickly steps in to escort him away from the field, having to kill some spaniards still attempting to attack the French monarch. Imperialist infantry mops up any remaining pockets of French troops still on the field, then retire to loot the French camp**

ROAD TO PAVIA

STREAM

08.00 **With the French king now under serious threat, his force being outnumbered three to one, Suffolk and Lorraine attempt an advance to support his position**

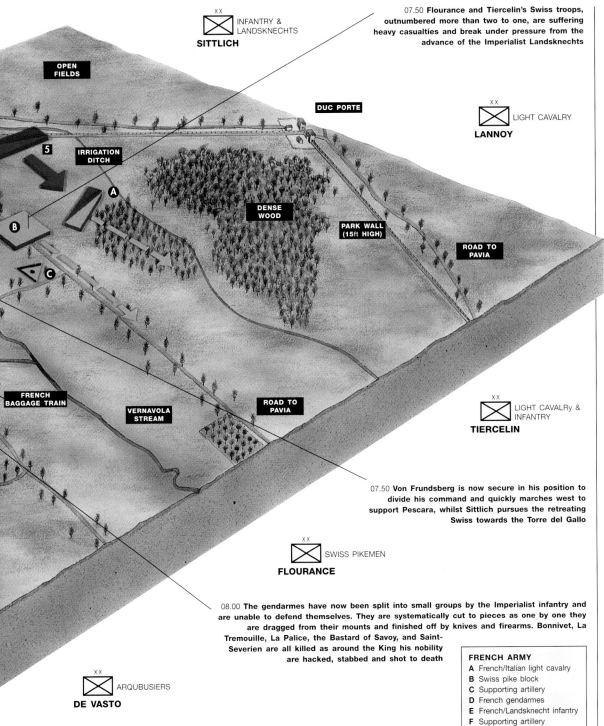

SITTLICH INFANTRY & LANDSKNECHTS
XX

07.50 **Flourance and Tiercelin's Swiss troops, outnumbered more than two to one, are suffering heavy casualties and break under pressure from the advance of the Imperialist Landsknechts**

OPEN FIELDS

DUC PORTE

LANNOY LIGHT CAVALRY
XX

5

IRRIGATION DITCH

A

DENSE WOOD

PARK WALL (15ft HIGH)

ROAD TO PAVIA

B

C

TIERCELIN LIGHT CAVALRy & INFANTRY
XX

FRENCH BAGGAGE TRAIN

VERNAVOLA STREAM

ROAD TO PAVIA

07.50 **Von Frundsberg is now secure in his position to divide his command and quickly marches west to support Pescara, whilst Sittlich pursues the retreating Swiss towards the Torre del Gallo**

FLOURANCE SWISS PIKEMEN
XX

08.00 **The gendarmes have now been split into small groups by the Imperialist infantry and are unable to defend themselves. They are systematically cut to pieces as one by one they are dragged from their mounts and finished off by knives and firearms. Bonnivet, La Tremouille, La Palice, the Bastard of Savoy, and Saint-Severien are all killed as around the King his nobility are hacked, stabbed and shot to death**

DE VASTO ARQUBUSIERS
XX

FRENCH ARMY
A French/Italian light cavalry
B Swiss pike block
C Supporting artillery
D French gendarmes
E French/Landsknecht infantry
F Supporting artillery

IMPERIALIST FORCES
1 Imperialist advances guard (arquebusiers)
2 Spanish/Landsknecht infantry
3 Landsknechts with supporting artillery
4/5 Imperialist light cavalry

BATTLE OF PAVIA

N

24th February 1525, viewed from the south, showing the developement of the Imperialist attack in the northern sector of Mirabello Park, the start of the French rout to the east, and their slaughter to the west leading to the capture of Francis I.

deployed the Imperialist foot (probably Spaniards) in the south of the wood so they faced the now immobile French horse. Spanish colunellas comprised a high proportion of arquebusiers, and these began firing on the French from the cover of the wood, supported by pikemen. Due to the terrain this would have been a scrappy affair: no clearly defined blocks of troops but rather a large number of men forced to fight in close combat and with little overall control. Once committed, this was a fight to the finish.

Frundsberg and Sittlich's Landsknechts had now been fighting the Swiss under Flourance for over an hour. The Swiss, outnumbered by more than two to one, had been getting the worst of it, and were being forced back. In some sources it is reported that the Swiss broke and ran; their lack of fight is attributed to lack of pay and poor morale. Although this may have been true in part, and the quitting of the Grisons before the battle does bear out this argument, the military reputation of the Swiss meant that this contest was far from one-sided. Whatever the true situation, things were going well enough for the Landsknecht commanders by the time Pescara's messenger arrived ordering them to detach half of their force (approximately one Fahnlein) and send it to Pescara's aid, with Frundsberg himself leading them. In all probability the Swiss were giving ground by this stage, retreating towards the Torre del Gallo, their force breaking up as it did so. D'Iespart, hero of the Binasco skirmish, was killed. Since the Imperialists listed both Flourance and the Swiss commander Jean von Diesbach among their prisoners, the situation might have been even worse; their commanders might already have been captured. Certainly the Landsknechts are credited with their capture, and if they were taken prisoner during the retreat of the Swiss towards the Ticino river, it is more likely that the credit for it would have gone to De Leyva's men.

THE FRENCH CAVALRY ARE ROUTED

While Frundsberg was regrouping his men and leading them through the woods towards the French cavalry, Bourbon, co-ordinating activities near the breaches, ordered a block of 4,000 Landsknechts against the left flank of the French cavalry and called up a reserve of 100 lances of Imperialist cavalry who were waiting north of the park. By 8am at the latest Francis and the French cavalry had found themselves virtually surrounded by Imperialist pikemen and arquebusiers, with no room to manoeuvre. The chroniclers (French sources in particular) describe the carnage in vivid detail. Although no doubt exaggerated, the scene must have been horrific, and the French cavalry, now outnumbered by more than three to one, began to get the worst of it. Many were knocked from their horses, and arquebusiers armed with knives or firearms finished them off. La Tremouille was killed by arquebusiers; apparently his body was riddled with metal splinters from his armour and lead from the firearms. Around the king the French nobility were gradually being hacked, stabbed or shot to death; those already killed included La Palice (Marishal of France), the Bastard of Savoy (Grand Master of France) and Saint-Severin (Master of the King's Horse), the last two of whom would have accompanied their monarch.

The French artillery, unable to fire in support of their king without firing on their own nobility, were forced to watch events unfold. Richard de la Pole, the Duke of Suffolk (an English exile), and Francois de Lorraine commanded the force of 4,000 Landsknechts in French service (the Black Band) and 2,000 French infantry. These now advanced to support the king, passing through the artillery battery. It is unclear whether they advanced directly ahead or angled to their left or right, but they were met by Frundsberg's Landsknechts and whatever troops Bourbon could spare. This was a private war, fought between Imperialist and French Landsknechts, where no quarter would be given or received. Bourbon's men-at-arms, unable to reach the French cavalry due to the press of Imperialist infantry, attacked in support of Frundsberg. From Frundsberg's account it appears that the French Landsknechts were marching to their left or front, since he records assaulting the enemy in their flank. The Black Band were heavily outnumbered but fought fiercely, reportedly dying where they stood.

To the east and 200 yards away the French cavalry were being cut to pieces, and a number of horsemen had begun to flee the field. The gendarmes forming the front line were bound by honour and social standing to remain fighting to the last, and in any event would have found it harder to extricate themselves than the lighter cavalry to their rear. At this point the king is reported to have exclaimed: 'My God! What is this?' By now his force had been split up into small groups of gendarmes, surrounded by Imperialist foot. Bonnivet (Admiral of France) was killed near the king, pierced by pikes although still astride his horse. In the middle of this carnage the king apparently fought well, until his horse was brought down and he was surrounded by arquebusiers armed with daggers. Lannoy, who by then had returned to the scene, is reputed to have ridden into the fray and rescued the king, defending him at sword point from his own men. French sources disagree, and a number of people claimed the glory of capturing the king. Whatever the situation, Lannoy was on hand to extricate the king and accompany him to the rear, escorted by files of Neapolitan arquebusiers (probably part of De Vasto's force). It has been claimed that the escort had to kill some Spanish troops who were still attempting to kill the French king.

As the French cavalry were either being slaughtered or routing, the Black Band were being cut down; their dead included Francois de Lorraine. Sources mention them

Jan Conelisz Vermeyen, The Conquest of Tunis, 1535, watercolour (detail).
(Kunsthistorisches Museum, Vienna) Fallen soldiers receiving a Christian burial amid the debris of the battlefield. Note the Turkish prisoners being rounded up in the background.

dying to a man, but in all likelihood many of them would also have broken, routing west towards the nearest corner of the park and safety. Frundsberg and Bourbon pursued, and were busy overrunning the French artillery when word was brought to them of the king's capture. Apparently Bourbon immediately rode off to meet his monarch, but was unable to find him.

To the east, Sittlich's Landsknechts had pursued the Swiss as far as the Torre de Gallo, where they overran the earthworks and captured the French artillery there and the French master of artillery, Galiot de Genoillac. By now aware that the Pavia garrison was occupying the southern corner of the park, the most likely direction for the Swiss rout was through the park gates at the Torre del Gallo, then south towards the five abbeys.

Around the five abbeys the Pavia garrison had attacked from the Toretta eastwards, rolling up the Swiss defensive positions. Unable to deploy in the boggy ground full of earthworks and the impedimenta of the siege, the 3,000 Swiss led by Montmorency were unable to stop the 9,000 men of the garrison. Under fire both from the Imperialist siege lines around the Casa del Levrieri and from the town itself, the Swiss finally broke when their compatriots reached them from the Torre del Gallo. This whole mass of men fled south, towards the boggy banks of the Ticino river. Some sources claim that the pontoon bridge there was cast adrift by the French troops on the south bank, following the orders of D'Alençon. This seems unlikely since D'Alençon was near San Lanfranco, to the west of the city, and had no clear idea of what was going on. If the bridge was destroyed it would have been on the authority of the local commander on the Borgo Ticino (the southern bank). Bridge or not, the mass of routing Swiss troops had problems crossing the swollen river, and many were drowned in the river or cut down by the Imperialist soldiers who pursued them down to the river-bank. Probably around half of the 5-6,000 Swiss troops on the north bank reached safety over the river.

The Duke of Alençon had realised that things were going badly in the park. His first indication of the Imperialist attack would have been the sounds of fighting in the park, almost 5,000 metres away to the north-east. A force of Italian light cavalry formed part of his command, and it is likely that scouts from this body would have brought him news of the full extent of the disaster at around 8.30am. This would have been confirmed by reports of routing troops fleeing westwards from the Porta Repentita and over the river in the Borgo Ticino. Without clear orders and unable to influence the outcome of the battle, he ordered a general retreat back towards Binasco and Milan, abandoning his siegeworks. This force constituted the last formed French troops left on the battlefield. By 9am at the latest the fighting was over. The Imperialist commanders were left on the battlefield amid the carnage and chaos of the shattered French army, trying to come to terms with the scale of their unexpected victory. Francis was being led to safety at the Imperialist headquarters at the Casa de Levrieri where his wounds were dressed, the survivors of the French army were in flight and the victors were enjoying the spoils of war and giving thanks that they were still alive. The battle that nobody had anticipated had ended with a result that nobody could have expected.

FRANCIS AND
HIS GENDARMES
Throughout the Italian wars the gendarmes (fully armoured noble cavalrymen) were the primary striking force in the French army. Protected by a full suit of plate armour, these horsemen were mounted on robust warhorses. The horses in turn wore protective plate armour over their head and neck and around their rump and front chest. Gendarmes were armed with a heavy iron-tipped wooden lance, a sword and often also a mace or axe. Armour was often of the highest quality, produced by the finest armourers in Italy and Germany. As the armour was often blackened, the rather foreboding appearance of horse and rider was augmented by coloured plumes, surcoats and horse bards.

When Francis I became aware of the Imperialist incursion into the park he ordered his cavalry to prepare for battle. Arms and armour scholars in the Tower of London estimate that even supposing the gendarmes slept fully dressed, the process of donning armour and readying for battle would have taken at least half an hour.

AFTERMATH

The French lost something in the region of 10,000 men in the Battle of Pavia, a relatively insignificant number when set against French losses during the Italian Wars as a whole. The main difference was that this time the dead included a large section of the French nobility, including Bonnivet, La Tremouille, La Palice, the Duke of Suffolk, Seigneur Lautrec de Foix, the Bastard of Savoy, Seigneur Francois de Lorraine and a string of lesser nobles.

This list was matched by that recording prisoners in Imperialist hands, some of them severely wounded. These included Flourance, Montmorency, Saluzzo, Henry of Navarre, Tiercelin, the Count of Saint-Pol, Galiot de Genouillac and numerous others.

Following a long-awaited meeting between Francis and Bourbon, Lannoy ensured that the king's wounds were dressed (he had been cut on the face and hands) and then took him to the Certosa di Pavia for the remainder of the day, well away from the carnage. There, Lannoy drafted a letter describing his victory to Charles V, and in return for safe conduct through France his messenger carried a note for Louise de Savoie (the French king's mother) which Francis began with the words:

'To inform you of how the rest of my ill-fortune is proceeding, all is lost to me save honour and life, which is safe.'

Within a few days Francis was removed to the fortress at Pizzighettone, safe from any attempt to rescue him or to kill him. Meanwhile, while the bodies of the French nobility were being sold by the soldiery to their French servants, colleagues or representatives of their families, dissension was growing in the Imperialist ranks. The mercenaries in the army had not been paid for some period before the battle, and the bad feelings this had engendered now came to a head. Four days after the battle the Landsknechts ignored the pleadings of Frundsberg and Sittlich and stormed the Imperialist headquarters, by then located in the Castello Visconti in Pavia. Lannoy had no money to pay them, but he was able to issue promissory notes drawn against his estates and those of Pescara and De Leyva. He managed to assuage the mercenaries, and the crisis passed. Lannoy then released his non-ransomable French prisoners and escorted them to the French frontier, a gruelling march in which many died from exposure and starvation. D'Alençon, on reaching Milan with the remains of the army rearguard, collected the garrison, apart from a body detailed off to hold the Castello for as long as possible. He then led a retreat back to the French frontier and in late March reached Lyons, where he died of pneumonia contracted during the retreat.

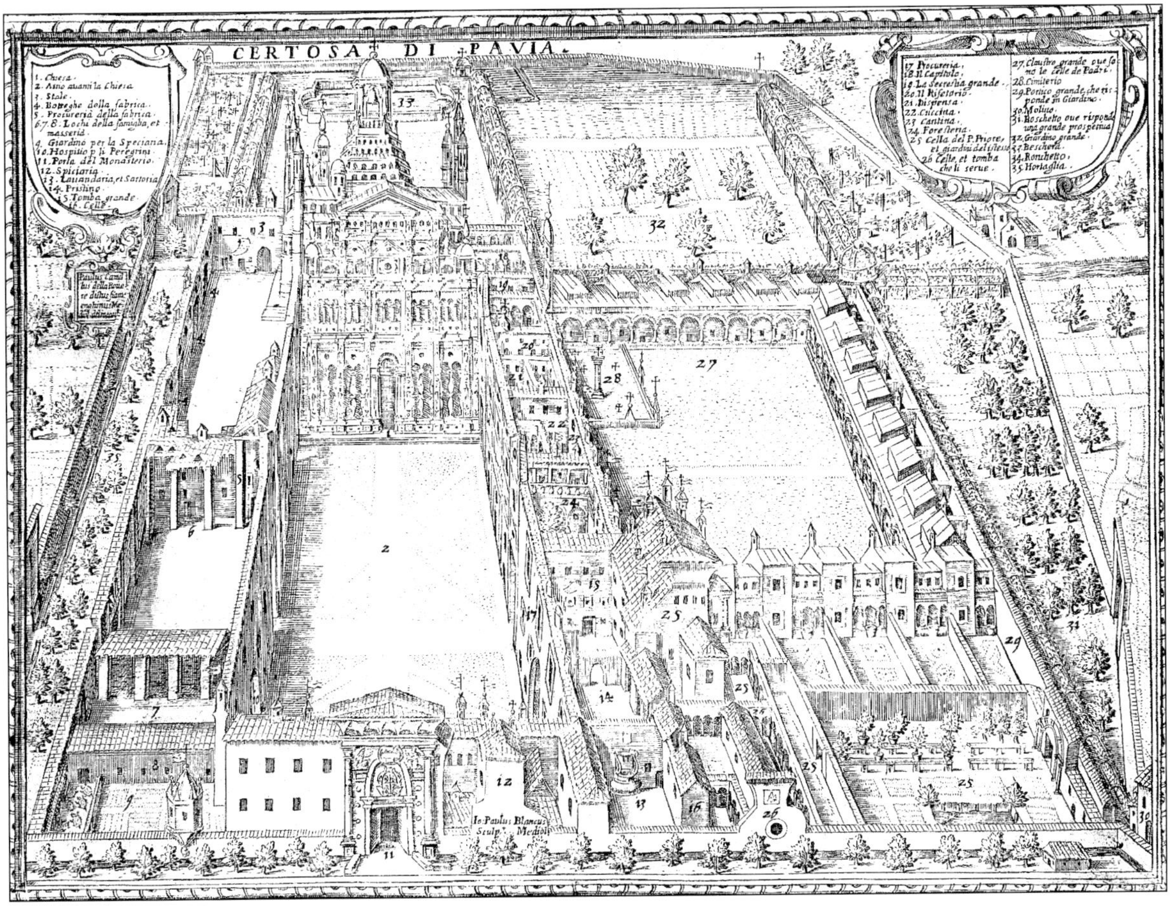

Paolo Camillo della Rovere, Certosa di Pavia, engraving, early 17th century. Following the battle, Francis I was taken here to have his wounds dressed and kept away from the roving bands of soldiers in the park after the battle. It was situated one mile north of the Porta Repentita.

Milan was occupied by Imperialist troops on 3 March, and Lannoy, Pescara and Bourbon moved their headquarters there as soon as was possible. The three commanders were only now coming to terms with the scale of their victory; an initial reticence and humility is reflected in their letters and dispatches. This was quickly replaced by attempts to explain their performance in the muddled battle, and to embellish the roles they played. Both Lannoy and Pescara praised Bourbon, Lannoy reporting that he 'had acquitted himself well and has indeed done his duty'. Pescara was more scathing of Lannoy's performance, calling him inept. Pescara's account of the battle also emphasised the part played by De Vasto, his nephew. In retrospect it is reasonably easy to agree with Pescara. While Lannoy had played little direct part in the operation of the battle and occupied himself by taking direct control of a cavalry body which was subsequently routed, his subordinates had performed well. Bourbon, Frundsberg and, perhaps especially, Pescara had been able to take stock of the developing situation and to respond to it, either steadying troops, moving them where they were needed or co-ordinating attacks. It is said that in every battle there comes a critical point where the battle could be lost or won depending on the decision of the commander. A good commander should know when this point has been reached and send in his reserves or take some similar decisive step. Pescara, on the spot and reading the battle well, realised this and acted accordingly. In this respect the Imperialist com-

PIKE FIGHT

Two major actions between opposing units of pikemen took place during the battle. The first involved a block of Imperialist Landsknechts against their Swiss counterparts, led by Flourance. This took place in the eastern section of the park. The second was fought between Imperialist Landsknechts and Landsknechts in French pay, who had defied the Imperial decree to decline French service. Both were deemed to be fought with particular ferocity, even by the standards of the time. In the second encounteby both sides - a true fight to the finish. The pike used at this stage of the Italian wars had reached a roughly standard length of around 16 feet. The theory that Landsknechts wielded shorter pikes is not borne out by an examination of contemporary inventories, illustrations and surviving examples. The Swiss were recorded to have held their in the middle of the haft rather than at the point of balance (approximately two-thirds down the haft). This was probably the result of their method of presenting the pike overarm rather than at shoulder heightr, quarter was denied.

Anonymous, although signed *'Na Dat', The Battle of Ravenna*, engraving, c.1512.
This shows French gendarmes preparing for battle, with more cavalry and Landsknechts in the background. The artillery piece in the foreground is an artistic convention, emphasising the role artillery played in the battle.

similar decisive step. Pescara, on the spot and reading the battle well, realised this and acted accordingly. In this respect the Imperialist commanders showed greater abilities than their French counterparts. While both sides were disorientated by the mist and unsure of enemy strengths and deployments, Pescara, Bourbon and Frundsberg were quick to realise that their raid was developing into a full-scale battle, and took advantage of their central position to defeat the enemy in detail.

Charles V and his court in Madrid received news of the victory on 10 March, and he then began to consider how his empire could take advantage of the unexpected situation. Bourbon's dispatch suggested that the victory should be followed up by an immediate invasion of southern France and that the alliance with England should be resurrected. The news had already reached London, where Henry VIII ordered a fireworks display in celebration. France appeared to be open for the taking. Neither monarch had reckoned on the abilities of the French king's mother.

While negotiations were opened between Francis and his captors, his mother busied herself shoring up the military and political defences of France. The Swiss mercenaries in French service or their families were paid in full, a move which contrasted well with the Imperialist attitude. This guaranteed their loyalty and ensured France's position

The French Army

7,000 Swiss mercenaries (including approximately 700 arquebusiers)
4,000 Landsknecht mercenaries (including approximately 500 arquebusiers)
4,000 French infantry (including approximately 2,000 arquebusiers)
2,000 Italian mercenaries (all arquebusiers)
2,000 French and Italian light cavalry
1,000 lances of gendarmes (1,000 gendarmes, 2,000 heavy cavalry, 1,000 light cavalry, 2,000 pages and servants)
Train of artillery

Dispositions

Flourance (at Torre del Gallo) 4,000 Swiss, 1,000 light cavalry, artillery
Francis I (at Porta Repentita) 900 lances, 2,000 French infantry, 4,000 Landsknechts, artillery
Montmorency (at five abbeys) 3,000 Swiss
Alençon (at San Lanfranco) 1,000 French infantry, 1,000 light cavalry, 2,000 Italians, artillery
(at Borgo Ticino) 100 lances, 1,000 French infantry

as a good mercenary employer. Next she rejected the conditions imposed by Charles V for her son's release, namely the handing over of Burgundy and the annexed Bourbon lands. Money was raised, the French survivors of her son's army were paid and reorganised in Lyons, and more troops were raised. While the Duke of Vendome organised the defences of Picardy against an expected English attack, she sent an embassy to Henry VIII's court to emphasise the danger of an overpowerful emperor.

On 10 June 1525 Francis was embarked on a Spanish galley at Genoa, escorted by a small fleet and shadowed by French warships. While it was made known that his destination was Naples, the king was taken instead to Barcelona, and then escorted overland to Madrid. He arrived there on 17 July, and negotiations on the terms of his release were begun in earnest.

The political situation was rapidly changing in France's favour. On 11 August a treaty was signed whereby Henry VIII would cancel any invasion of France and petition for the release of Francis in return for substantial financial gain. The English change of attitude was the result of increasing anxiety at the thought of a powerful Spain and Empire, and partly because any invasion of Picardy would now prove difficult and costly, with no guarantee of success. The Regent Louise had quickly secured her northern borders. At the same time, word reached Charles V of an anti-Imperialist alliance in Italy, led by the Pope and supported by Venice, Florence and a number of other minor states.

Following a meeting between Francis I and Charles V in mid-September, ambassadors of both sides sat down to negotiate. This resulted in the signing of the Treaty of Madrid, on 14 January 1526. The terms were that Francis I would cede Burgundy to Charles V and marry the emperor's

Anonymous, The Exchange of Francis I for his two sons, 1526, woodcut, early 17th century. (Bibliotheque National, Paris)
French representatives approach the king escorted by Lannoy in this exchange at Bidassoa, on the Spanish-French border.

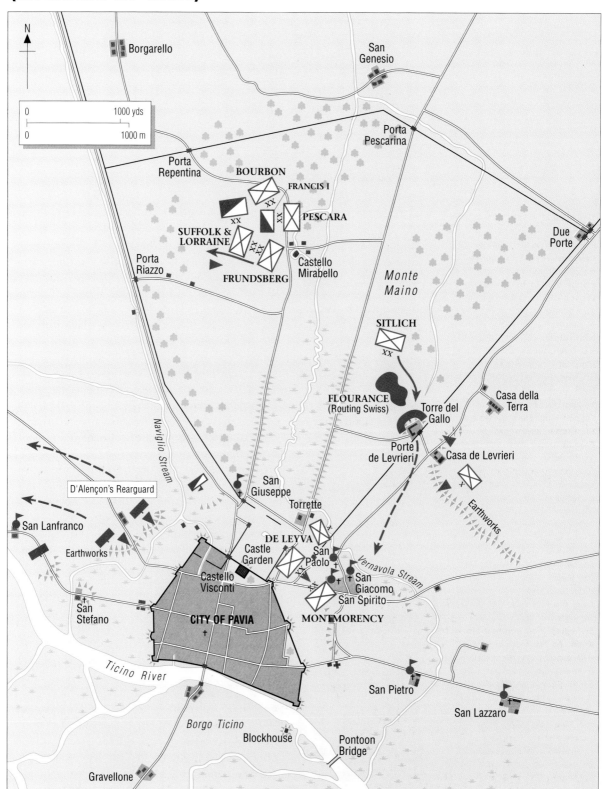

N

0 — 1000 yds
0 — 1000 m

Borgarello

San Genesio

Porta Pescarina

Porta Repentina

BOURBON

FRANCIS I

PESCARA

SUFFOLK & LORRAINE

Porta Riazzo

FRUNDSBERG

Castello Mirabello

Monte Maino

Due Porte

SITLICH

Casa della Terra

FLOURANCE
(Routing Swiss)

Torre del Gallo

Casa de Levrieri

Porte de Levrieri

Earthworks

Naviglio Stream

San Giuseppe

Torrette

D'Alençon's Rearguard

San Lanfranco

Earthworks

DE LEYVA

Castle Garden

San Paolo

San Giacomo

San Spirito

Vernavola Stream

Castello Visconti

CITY OF PAVIA

MONTEMORENCY

San Stefano

Ticino River

San Pietro

San Lazzaro

Borgo Ticino

Blockhouse

Pontoon Bridge

Gravellone

The closing stages of the battle. Following the charge of Francis I and the French cavalry, Pescara ordered the concentration of all available Imperialist troops around the flailing French cavalry. This concentration was assisted by the defeat of Flourance's Swiss pikemen, who retreated towards the Torre del Gallo, pursued by a detachment of Landsknechts. This allowed Frundsberg to regroup a large portion of his troops and to join in the attack on the French king. Here he was able to counter an attempt by the French to cut their way through to the king, the attempt resulting in the bloody fight between Landsknechts in Imperial and French service. Meanwhile, De Leyva and the Pavia garrison attacked the Swiss in their positions around the 'five abbeys'. Without the space to deploy in formation, the Swiss pikemen were defeated. Swiss troops, routing from the Torre del Gallo, poured through the 'five abbeys', sweeping their compatriots with them. As the last pockets of resistance were being crushed in the north of the park, the Swiss portion of the army flooded from the field, heading for the pontoon bridges over the Ticino river. As word reached D'Alençon of the defeat of the king he began an orderly retreat to the north-west, screening the routing army from Imperialist attack.

pensation both for his lost French lands and for the crown of Portugal. As a hostage until the handover of Burgundy could be achieved, Francis was required to place his two eldest sons in the emperor's hands for safe-keeping. On 17 March the king was escorted over the Spanish-French border at Bidassoa, in exchange for his sons.

Francis had no intention of weakening his position by handing over Burgundy, and by 22 May he had obtained a release, signed by the Pope, from his moral obligations of carrying out the terms of the Treaty of Madrid. What France had lost on the battlefield had been recovered by deceit and diplomacy.

Warfare continued in Italy for a further four years. In 1527 a fresh French expedition led by Lautrec besieged Pavia and sacked the city before being forced to withdraw from Italy the following year. A fresh Imperialist army quelled the revolt of the Italian states, a campaign culminating in the sack of Rome in May 1527. Italy had been subjected to the horrors of almost continual warfare since 1494, and the drain on both Imperialist and French resources had been considerable. At the same time, Charles V, as Holy Roman Emperor, had to deal with a Turkish army which was besieging Vienna and a looming Protestant rebellion in Germany. So when Francis asked to discuss peace terms, Charles agreed, and the talks resulted in the Treaty of Cambrai, signed in 1529, which brought an end to the war in Italy. France gave up her claims in Italy and paid substantial war reparations. In return, Charles abandoned his demand for Burgundy and returned the French king's sons unharmed.

Although the war between France and the Empire would continue intermittently for a further 20 years, the Empire would never again grasp and then lose such a marvellous opportunity as that which fell into its hands at Pavia.

The Imperialists

12,000 Landsknecht mercenaries (including approximately 1,500 arquebusiers)
5,000 Spanish infantry (including approximately 1,700 arquebusiers)
3,000 Italian infantry (all arquebusiers)
800 lances
1,500 Spanish and Italian light cavalry
Artillery and engineers

De Leyva's Garrison

3,000 Spanish infantry (including approximately 1,000 arquebusiers)
7,000 Landsknecht (including approximately 800 arquebusiers)
30 lances of Spanish men-at-arms
1,000 armed city militia
Small train of artillery

Dispositions

Garrison sortie group: (De Leyva) 3,000 Spanish infantry, 7,000 Landsknecht mercenaries
Raiding party: (De Vasto) 3,000 Italian arquebusiers
Supporting group: (Lannoy and Pescara) 1,000 light cavalry, artillery
Reserve support group: (Pescara, Bourbon, Frundsberg and Sittlich) 4,000 Spanish infantry, 12,000 Landsknecht mercenaries
Final reserve: 800 lances
Garrison: 1,000 city militia, 30 lances
Camp garrison: 1,000 Spanish infantry, artillery train

THE BATTLEFIELD TODAY

The railway came to Pavia in the mid-19th century, the line from Milan cutting through the battlefield from north to south until it reaches Pavia station, built on the ground where the French siege lines once stood, to the east of the old city walls. With the city growth encountered during the Industrial Revolution, Pavia expanded beyond its old city walls; new suburbs sprang up in all directions, particularly towards the east and west. The Vernavola stream still follows much the same course it did in 1525, running southwards past the now sprawling farming village of Mirabello then snaking its way towards and around the city until it merges with the Ticino river about a mile to the east of its original course. Its banks have been drained since the 16th century, and it's direction now flows through prime agricultural meadowland until it reaches the city suburbs near the start of the five abbeys complex.

The abbey buildings still exist in a reduced form, although later modifications make it difficult to determine the extent of the 16th-century buildings, walls and orchards. When walking the ground, it is reasonably clear what an excellent defensive position these made: a slight rise from the Vernavola gives the defenders a clear field of fire over the stream and the far bank. To the west of the town another slight rise beyond the railway station provides a good firing position for any attacker, and judging by the location of the French artillery battery in the fresco in San Theodoro, in the centre of Pavia, this was where the French placed their siege battery which bombarded the western town wall. This slight ridge is now covered in buildings, including a vast hospital complex and a network of 19th-century houses and factories.

The old Visconti park walls have long since been demolished, and only traces of the original city walls can be found, near the Castello de Visconti and at the north-western corner, where the 16th-century tower has been replaced by an artillery bastion. To the east, the line of the park wall can be traced by field boundaries, although the road to Lardirago follows the same route it took in 1525, when the Imperialists used it for their night march. It still passes between the Torre del Gallo and the Casa del Levrieri, both of which are now small farms. To the west, the line of the park wall can be traced by the line of the Navaglio canal until it turns west, following the line of the present-day track to the Casa Repentita and San Ginesio, which is now another sprawling farming village. The Casa Repentita is purportedly built upon the site of the falconry mews which Francis I had constructed during the siege.

The railway crosses the line of the old park wall at Repentita, then continues north through what was the new park until it reaches the

Holbein the Younger, *Infantry Battle*, drawing (detail), c.1530. (Kunstmuseum, Basle)
One of two matching drawings, in this illustration Swiss pikemen are shown in combat with Landsknechts, the Swiss troops carrying halberds, two-handed swords and Lucerne hammers as well as pikes. The ferocity and confusion of the struggle is vividly portrayed.

Certosa di Pavia, now served by a small station. The railway bisects the deployment area of the king, his cavalry, Landsknechts and their attendant artillery battery. Traces of the substantial woods around the Porta Pescarina and the Torre del Gallo can still be seen, but they have been reduced by farming activity to just a scattering of little copses. Otherwise the park is little altered apart from drainage and the addition of more farm-related buildings. It still gives the impression of being as flat as a billiard table, and with a little imagination the visitor can picture what it would have looked like in 1525.

During a recent visit to the battlefield the author had the unexpected bonus of encountering the thick morning mist which cloaked the battlefield in 1525. For the record, this lasted from dawn until 10am, and according to locals this is an almost daily occurrence throughout the winter. With visibility down to around 100 metres it is easy to see how two armies could blunder about in close proximity to each other without knowing what the other was doing. Given the battlefield control at the time, the thick mist, the broken-up terrain and the scattered deployments, it isn't hard to feel a little sorry for Francis I!

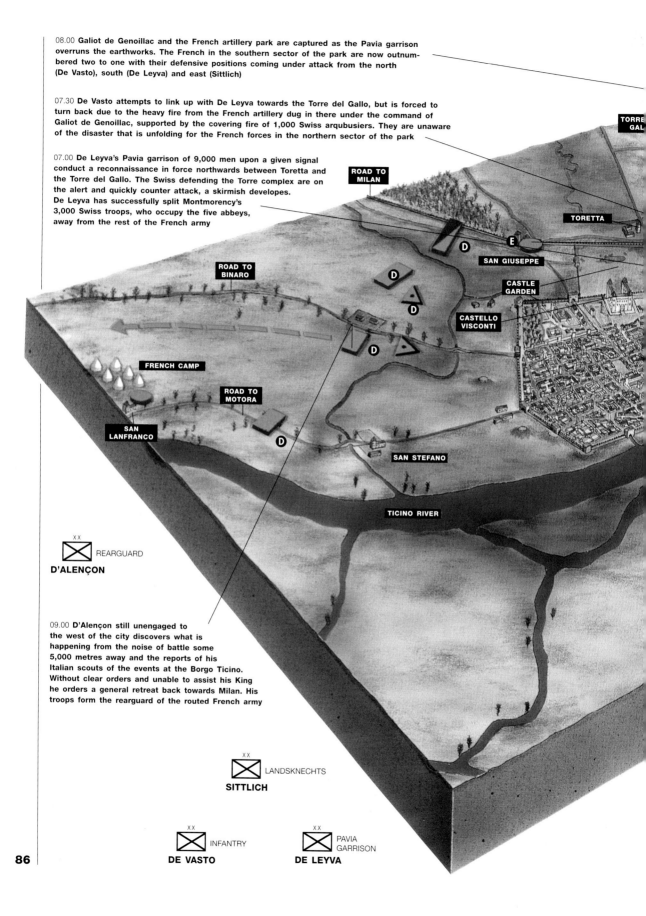

08.00 **Galiot de Genoillac** and the French artillery park are captured as the Pavia garrison overruns the earthworks. The French in the southern sector of the park are now outnumbered two to one with their defensive positions coming under attack from the north (De Vasto), south (De Leyva) and east (Sittlich)

07.30 **De Vasto** attempts to link up with De Leyva towards the Torre del Gallo, but is forced to turn back due to the heavy fire from the French artillery dug in there under the command of Galiot de Genoillac, supported by the covering fire of 1,000 Swiss arqubusiers. They are unaware of the disaster that is unfolding for the French forces in the northern sector of the park

07.00 **De Leyva's** Pavia garrison of 9,000 men upon a given signal conduct a reconnaissance in force northwards between Toretta and the Torre del Gallo. The Swiss defending the Torre complex are on the alert and quickly counter attack, a skirmish developes. De Leyva has successfully split Montmorency's 3,000 Swiss troops, who occupy the five abbeys, away from the rest of the French army

TORRE GAL

ROAD TO MILAN

TORETTA

D

E

SAN GIUSEPPE

D

CASTLE GARDEN

D

CASTELLO VISCONTI

ROAD TO BINARO

D

D

FRENCH CAMP

ROAD TO MOTORA

D

SAN LANFRANCO

D

SAN STEFANO

TICINO RIVER

x x
REARGUARD
D'ALENÇON

09.00 **D'Alençon** still unengaged to the west of the city discovers what is happening from the noise of battle some 5,000 metres away and the reports of his Italian scouts of the events at the Borgo Ticino. Without clear orders and unable to assist his King he orders a general retreat back towards Milan. His troops form the rearguard of the routed French army

x x
LANDSKNECHTS
SITTLICH

x x
INFANTRY
DE VASTO

x x
PAVIA GARRISON
DE LEYVA

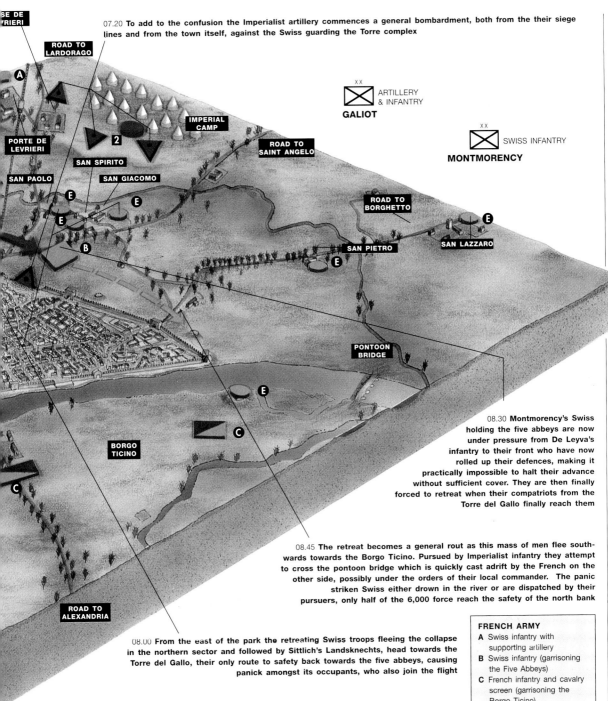

07.20 To add to the confusion the Imperialist artillery commences a general bombardment, both from the their siege lines and from the town itself, against the Swiss guarding the Torre complex

SE DE RIERI

ROAD TO LARDORAGO

Ⓐ

PORTE DE LEVRIERI

IMPERIAL CAMP

SAN SPIRITO

2

ROAD TO SAINT ANGELO

SAN PAOLO

SAN GIACOMO

Ⓔ

Ⓔ

Ⓔ

Ⓑ

SAN PIETRO

Ⓔ

ROAD TO BORGHETTO

SAN LAZZARO

Ⓔ

x x

⊠ ARTILLERY & INFANTRY

GALIOT

x x

⊠ SWISS INFANTRY

MONTMORENCY

PONTOON BRIDGE

Ⓔ

BORGO TICINO

Ⓒ

Ⓒ

ROAD TO ALEXANDRIA

08.30 Montmorency's Swiss holding the five abbeys are now under pressure from De Leyva's infantry to their front who have now rolled up their defences, making it practically impossible to halt their advance without sufficient cover. They are then finally forced to retreat when their compatriots from the Torre del Gallo finally reach them

08.45 The retreat becomes a general rout as this mass of men flee southwards towards the Borgo Ticino. Pursued by Imperialist infantry they attempt to cross the pontoon bridge which is quickly cast adrift by the French on the other side, possibly under the orders of their local commander. The panic striken Swiss either drown in the river or are dispatched by their pursuers, only half of the 6,000 force reach the safety of the north bank

08.00 From the east of the park the retreating Swiss troops fleeing the collapse in the northern sector and followed by Sittlich's Landsknechts, head towards the Torre del Gallo, their only route to safety back towards the five abbeys, causing panick amongst its occupants, who also join the flight

BATTLE OF PAVIA

Viewed from the south showing the sortie of the Pavia garrison, launching an attack against the French siege positions and the five abbeys occupied by the Swiss, which culminates in the total rout of Francis's forces back towards Milan. (06.00 - 09.00)

N

FRENCH ARMY
A Swiss infantry with supporting artillery
B Swiss infantry (garrisoning the Five Abbeys)
C French infantry and cavalry screen (garrisoning the Borgo Ticino)
D French/Italian infantry and light cavalry (garrisoning the area around San Lanfranco)
E French garrisons

IMPERIALIST FORCES
1 Pavia garrison supported by artillery in the city defences
2 Imperialist camp garrison and main artillery park

CHRONOLOGY

1514

31 December – Death of Louis XII; accession of Francis I as king of France

1515

13-14 September – Battle of Marignano; French victory

1519

12 January – Death of the emperor Maximilian I
28 June – Election of Charles of Austria, king of Spain, as Holy Roman Emperor

1520

6 June – Meeting between Francis I and Henry VIII at the Field of the Cloth of Gold

1521

March – War breaks out between France and the Empire
28 November – Emperor, Pope and Henry VIII sign alliance against Francis I

1522

29 April – Battle of La Bicocca; French defeat

1523

18 July – Agreement signed between the Duke of Bourbon and Charles V
11 September – Plot discovered and Bourbon forced to flee from France
October – Bonnivet invades Italy
28 December – Death of Colonna; Lannoy becomes Imperialist commander in Italy

1524

April – Bonnivet retreats over French border
July – Imperialist army invades Provence
mid-August – Marseilles besieged
21 September – Imperialists raise siege and retreat back to Italy; Francis I pursues the Imperialist army into Italy
26 October Milan captured by the French
28 October Siege of Pavia begins
21 November – Two-pronged assault on city repulsed
12 December – Secret treaty signed between Pope and Francis I
mid-December – Operations around Piacenza

1525

10 January – Landsknecht reinforcements arrive in Imperialist camp
24-25 January – Operations around San Angelo

3 February – Imperialist army arrives and fortifies itself in positions facing the French siege lines at Pavia
19-22 February – Imperialists reconnoitre the park
23 February 22:00 – mperialists begin approach march
24 February –
  00:00 Imperialist army arrives in front of breach
  05:00 De Vasto and his arquebusiers enter park; Flourance's Swiss move north to investigate
  05:30 Cavalry skirmish near the Porta Pescarina; Swiss overrun Imperialist artillery
  06:00 Signal made to launch sortie by garrison
  06:30 Mirabello stormed by De Vasto; main Imperialist army enters park
  07:00 Clash between Frundsberg's Landsknechts and Flourance's Swiss; Pavia garrison sorties and captures the Toretta
  07:20 French artillery batteries open up on Imperialist infantry
  07:40 Francis I launches cavalry charge and routs Imperialist cavalry
  07:50 Pescara recalls De Vasto and requests reinforcements; Flourance's Swiss begin to break
  08:00 French cavalry surrounded; Landsknechts in French pay advance in support of king
  08:15 Fight between Suffolk's Landsknechts and those of Frundsberg
  08:20 Francis I captured; French cavalry destroyed
  08:30 Rout of Swiss around the five abbeys; general rout towards the Ticino river
  09:00 The Duc d'Alençon withdraws from the field, ending the battle
26 February – Francis I imprisoned in fortress of Pizzighettone
3 March – Milan occupied
10 March – The news of the Imperialist victory reaches Madrid
12 July – Francis I arrives in Madrid and is imprisoned

1526

14 January – The Treaty of Madrid is signed
17 March – Francis I is exchanged for his sons and returns to French soil
22 May – Francis I repudiates the treaty, with the Pope's blessing

1527

May – Rome is sacked; Bourbon is killed in the attack

1529

Treaty of Cambrai ends the Italian Wars

1547

Francis I dies

WARGAMING PAVIA

Pavia is a complex battle which takes a degree of ingenuity to wargame properly. One project which immediately entranced me was the idea of taking the Bird's-Eye-Views of the entire city as a whole, enlarging it with a photocopier, drawing a grid over it and fighting out the entire battle. One method would be to use 2mm or 6mm figures as counters. Using hidden movement on the grid with a DBA-style command system avoids having to work out who can hear the guns or keeping track of messengers. Once opposing counters meet then move to a wargames table and replace the counters with the relevant figures. Using this system you include D'Alençon and Montmorency's troops as well as the garrison's sally. However, if you just want a one-night battle, things are more simple. You only really want to concentrate on the vital part of the engagement - the fighting which took place in the park.

Having chosen the action to be fought, the size of the figures you use does not really matter. To a great extent this is also true of the rules. Provided you have a reasonable set of rules which competently cover the period you shouldn't have any problems. Where the rules will be tested is in their ability to cope with hidden movement.

Every battle has something which has to be included in the game if the game is to make any pretence at resembling the historical reality. In the case of Pavia it is the poor visibility and cluttered terrain which split the battle up into several separate actions and meant that no one really knew what was going on. This aspect must somehow be recreated in the game.

After setting out the terrain create a grid on the wargames table. This can easily be done by sticking drawing pins along all four edges, 6ins. apart and using them to anchor cotton, string or wool drawn across the table to produce a grid with 6in. squares. Number each square, the numbers corresponding to those in a matchbox grid. The matchbox grid is an old wargamers' device; simply stick empty matchboxes together edge-to-edge so that they form a rectangular block of similar proportions to your wargames table. Make sure each drawer can open and label each drawer so that it corresponds to one square of the grid on the wargames table. When a unit moves from one square to another on the table it does not need to physically appear on the table at all; the movement can be represented by moving a counter from one tray to another in the matchbox grid. Simply move the troops using counters in the matchbox trays. Both players can move their troops using the same method. If one player opens a tray to put a counter in and finds an enemy counter already in place they have made

THE CAPTURE OF FRANCIS I

Following the charge of Francis I at the head of his gendarmes, the French cavalry found themselves hemmed in by the open wood of the central park and the Vernavola stream with its attendant boggy ground and drainage ditches. Pinned to the front by pikemen and surrounded by an ever growing body of arquebusiers, the French nobility found themselves surrounded, with no room to manoeuvre. The rash charge had left them completely at the mercy of the Imperialist infantry. Lances, useless at close quarters, were abandoned in favour of swords and maces. The accounts of both French and Imperialist participants describe the carnage that followed. Riders were pulled from their horses and decapitated, arquebusiers thrust their firearms into gaps in the gendarmes' plate armour and fired, causing horrific injuries. Other nobles were found riddled with pike and bullet wounds, and in at least one case the rider remained upright on his horse, the press of men preventing him from falling to the ground.

Francis I was unhorsed and only the rapid arrival of senior Imperialist officers prevented him from being hacked to death.

Barnaert van Orley, *The Pavia Tapestry*, c.1531. (Capodimonte, Naples) A detail of one of the small 'pillbox'-shaped block-houses employed during the siege. Constructed by De Leyva and the Pavia garrison, by the time of the battle many of them were in French hands.

contact and those figures represented by the counters in that matchbox tray are placed on the wargames table in the appropriate grid square.

Using 6in. grid squares has several advantages. It is a convenient size for movement, avoiding the need to worry about the movement rates of different troop types. All units move 6ins. or one grid square per move. This is a convenient way of enforcing night movement rules, none of the units knew exactly where they were or what was going on, and no commander in his right mind is going to move around at full speed in such conditions. It also effectively restricts visibility and makes it harder to avoid troops bumping into each other.

An alternative method for hidden movement is to use two tables. One table covers the area between the French camp and the Vernavola stream, which is Francis's battlefield. The other table covers the area between the Vernavola stream and the irrigation ditch which is Flourance's battlefield. Either hang a curtain between the two tables or place them some distance apart. The battle was split into two and the participants on one side of the wood didn't know what was happening on the other side of the wood. Physically splitting the battlefield so that the players only see their own troops gives the French some much-needed help. If Imperialist players can see the whole situation they are very rational about shifting troops from one action to another. However, if they don't know just how the battle is progressing elsewhere they can become altogether more parochial. The hidden movement engenders a mild paranoia and everyone fears that they have not yet found the greatest enemy threat.

A hidden movement system addresses some of the realism issues but it leaves the problem of how to encourage the players to behave like their predecessors. The first step is to conceal from the players which particular engagement they are fighting. If the players know which battle they are involved in they will actively seek to avoid the errors of their historical counterparts. Tell them that you are trying to refight an incident from the siege of Pavia. The French should be told that raids, sorties and attempts to push supplies through to the garrison are all part of the daily grind and nothing special. The Imperialists should be gathered together and told that they are to try to get pay through to the garrison. Either give them orders in writing or, wearing your hat as Charles V, tell them what they are to do. Hence De Vastos will be told to push through to Castello Mirabello with all speed prior to linking up with a force coming out of the town. (Obviously there is no such force but by the time that is realised he will be available to support Pescara.) Pescara and Lannoy are told to cover De Vastos' flank, exiting the woods and covering his line of advance and/or retreat. Frundsberg is told to do the same with the other flank, it being vital that enemy forces be kept from cutting the Imperialist line of retreat through the gaps in the wall. Bourbon is given a more flexible brief of supporting those who need it and grabbing any advantage that appears.

By stressing phrases such as 'raid', 'resupplying the garrison' and 'lines of retreat', you can hopefully get them to adopt a mind set similar to the original participants who were not at all expecting to fight and win one of the most important battles of the Italian wars. As a result they should behave very much like their predecessors. After the start it would be unfair to fetter them further with more orders. Historically, at some point, the original Imperialist commanders had the vision to overstep their orders and win a great battle. Your players should be allowed the same opportunity.

Another important factor is the timetable for the arrival of troops onto the table. The following schedule should give a realistic result. Where units arrive on the table is shown on the Bird's-Eye-Views.

Move 1 De Vastos Arquebusiers and Tiercelins light horse move onto the table

Move 2 Flourance and the Imperialist cavalry and guns arrive on table

Move 3 Pescara and Lannoy's troops arrive

Move 4 Sittlich arrives with first third of the Landsknechts

Move 5 Francis and his 900 lances deploy out of the camp

Move 6 Frundsberg and the next third of the Landsknechts arrive

Move 7 Suffolk with the French infantry and Landsknechts deploy out of the French camp

Move 8 Bourbon and the last third of the Landsknechts arrive

Move 9 Final Imperialist reserve of 800 lances arrives.

Remember, these don't actually appear on the table. They are moved secretly in the matchbox grid until they make contact. This means that no one really knows what is going on or where other units are. This is the only hope that Flourance's Swiss have of surviving, but hopefully they will not realise this.

When fighting the battle we introduced a few 'house rules' to try to capture the flavour of the battle. Where Landsknechts meet hostile Landsknechts or Swiss they will attack immediately. Not only that, but in these combats, all combatants will follow retreating or recoiling opponents by the maximum extent allowed by the rules. If the rules you use don't allow for this, then I'd be tempted to write in a quick amendment to allow it. We found that it resulted, in the kind of savage hand-to-hand fighting reported at the time.

Other than this, there were no other rule changes we felt were essential. However, a few tips to bear in mind: a word to any putative Pescara. Ours allowed his Spanish infantry to be lured out of the woods to support what remained of Lannoy's cavalry. Caught front, side and rear by enraged Gendarmes his force was virtually exterminated. Some sound advice is to hide in the woods until your arquebusiers have whittled the Gendarmes down and Frundsberg and his Landsknechts arrive.

Terrain plays a vital part in this game. The woods that matter are mainly open. They should not affect movement at all, but they do give infantry a bonus when fighting cavalry. Hence they provide a safe haven for the Imperialist troops should they care to use it. Castello Mirabello should be a small cluster of buildings without defenders. It protects the arquebusiers from the French Cavalry and allows them to outflank the Gendarmes as they face off Pescara's Spanish. In our game De Vasto led his men out of this shelter to try to rescue Pescara. He too discovered that Gendarmes in the open are a very different proposition to Gendarmes when you are hiding in the woods.

There is one particular 'What if' with regard to the battle that has an enduring fascination. Where did D'Alençon get to? Looked at dispassionately D'Alençon behaved sensibly. Whether as a result of doubts of his own ability or a good grasp of the situation he saved part of the army. However, what would have happened if he had chanced everything on a final throw? He would have been able to bring his troops from San Lanfranco into action; those at Borgo Ticino are just too far away to become involved. If you want to have D'Alençon coming to the rescue then have his troops enter along the Castello Mirabello Road where it runs parallel to the Vernavola stream. If you continue with hidden movement and the matchbox grid, he and his men could come as an unpleasant surprise to De Vasto's arquebusiers who have probably got their backs to Castello Mirabello.

Another much less likely 'What If' concerns a possible intervention by Montmorency. This assumes that the garrison's sally had either been turned back, perhaps by Montmorency catching them on the difficult ground they trapped him on, or more probably the sally was late or abandoned for some reason. If you want Montmorency to arrive having administered a salutary thrashing to a presumptuous garrison have him arrive on move 12 with 2,000 Swiss. If it makes any difference to the rules you could have his advance preceded by a screen of routers, the remnants of the garrison. A more likely option is that the sally never takes place. In this case, Montmorency should arrive with 3,000 Swiss on move eight. This may seem a little early but it will force a radical re-think on the part of Frundsberg.

Obviously the greatest 'What if' is to use the Bird's-Eye-View of the entire city to re-fight the whole engagement. You can then plan the entire operation from scratch, although you may find it difficult to come up with a better plan. Not only did the original prove extremely effective but it actually produces a very interesting game, as I hope you will find.

**Anonymous, The Battle of Pavia, 1525, oil painting,
c.1525-30. (Royal Armouries, Leeds)**
Similar to the Ashmoelean representation of the battle, it
is unclear which of the two paintings was produced first.
Clearly both are by the same artist, although in this case
the captions are written in Italian. In the foreground
Francis I clashes with Lannoy's cavalry. The middle distance shows the Imperialist infantry passing through the
breach, with siege works in the background, and in the
upper left corner French troops are shown fleeing the
battle.

FUTHER READING

Taylor, F., *The Art of War in Italy* (London 1921, reprinted 1993)
Oman, C., *A History of the Art of War in the Sixteenth Century* (1937, reprinted 1991)
Giono, J., *The Battle of Pavia, 24 February 1525* (Paris 1963, trans. London 1965)
Pitts, V.J., *The Man who sacked Rome* (Charles de Bourbon) (New York 1993)
Seward, D., *Prince of the Renaissance, the Life of Francis I* (London 1973)
Reinhard, B., *Georg von Frundsberg* (Munich 1988)

Note on Original Sources

Although a number of contemporary or near-contemporary accounts of the battle have been written, the majority are vague and self-congratulating, and almost all contradict one another. Therefore, any attempt to reconstruct the events of 24 February 1525 is an interpretation that could differ from reconstructions posed by other historians. The fundamental geographical errors in Oman's interpretation have caused confusion in general works such as Seward and Pitts. The work conducted by Reihard Thom, Die Schlacht bei Pavia (PhD thesis, Berlin 1907), presents a further interpretation. In this reconstruction the author has used the accounts of Pescara and the Abbe de Najera (imperial treasurer in the army) as well as the following published sources, placing the greater emphasis on the accounts of Frundsberg, Pescara and Flourance:

Flourance, R. de la Marck, *Memoires du Marechal de Flourance,* reproduced by Goubaux & Lemoisne (Paris 1913-24) 2 vols.

von Frundsberg, G., *Report on the battle of Pavia,* reproduced in Buchholz, *Geschichte der Regierung des Ferdinand I* (Hamburg 1883) Vol. IX.

Du Bellay, Martin & Guillaume, *Memoires de Martin et Guillaume du Bellay*, reproduced by Bourrilly & Vindry (Paris 1908, 1910) 2 vols.

Guicciardini, Fr., *The History of Italy from the year 1490 to 1532*, reproduced by Goddard (London 1753-56) 20 vols.

Moreau, S., *La Prince et Deliverance du Roy*, reproduced in *Archives Cuirasses* (Paris) Vol. II.